A YEAR OF INCREASING
WISDOM, STATURE, AND FAVOR

GREG AMUNDSON

EAGLE RISE SPEAKERS
——— B U R E A U ———

Above All Else

A YEAR OF INCREASING WISDOM, STATURE, AND FAVOR

By Greg Amundson
3703 Portola Drive, Santa Cruz, CA 95060
www.GregoryAmundson.com

Published by
Eagle Rise Speakers Bureau
Virginia Beach, Virginia, 2018

Edited by Patti Bond
Layout and Design by Brooktown Design, www.brooktown.com

ISBN 9781720295242
ASIN B07HBNKVM7

Legal Disclaimer by the Author:

The Author has done his best to articulate God's Law through interpretation of Bible Verse, Prayer, Meditation and Reflection. Unless otherwise noted, Scripture quotations are taken from the Holy Bible, New International Version, and King James Version.
Italics within the body of the daily devotionals signify either a direct Bible Verse, or a paraphrased verse. The visual stories contained in this devotional are from the authors imagination, or were retold from military leadership courses, the authors parents, or Church services at Twin Lakes Church in Aptos, California, or Presentation Church in Stockton, California.

Printed and bound in the USA and UK on acid-free paper.

PRAISE FOR THE WORK OF GREG AMUNDSON

"I often tell people at my seminars, 'We don't need more Buddhists in the world, we need more Buddhas. We don't need more Christians, we need more Christ-like beings.' And such is the case with my amazing, breathing brother Greg Amundson. He's not one of those wishy-washy, praise the Lord, in-your-face, superficial Christians: He is a former SWAT Operator, DEA Special Agent, U.S. Army Captain, and CrossFit athlete and coach. He is a spiritual warrior, and he carries God in his heart. Greg's books, *The Warrior and The Monk*, and *Above All Else*, are two of those books you can open and find pure inspiration." – *Dan Brulé*, world renowned lecturer and international bestselling author of *Just Breath*

"Sometimes our mythic roots carry the most powerful insights, and Greg Amundson's fable, *The Warrior and The Monk*, is no exception. Greg leverages his remarkable storytelling ability to help the reader acquire new insights that serve to strengthen the spiritual core. Greg's new book, *Above All Else*, provides me with daily wisdom, revelation, and greater understanding of God's Word, in a way that only Greg can provide. It's a game changer." – *Josh Mantz*, Former Army Major and #1 Amazon bestselling author of *The Beauty of a Darker Soul*

"Greg fought the war on drugs, battled in the streets, on behalf of our nation. Now he fights to inspire us to overcome our fears, flaws, and failures, battling for the glory of God. Pick up, *Above All Else*, and *The Warrior and The Monk*, and let God's work, through Greg's words and stories, uplift your mind, body and soul." – *Jay Dobyns*, author of *The New York Times* bestseller *No Angel,* and *Catching Hell*

"Greg's ability to transcend boundaries and speak to the essence of spirituality is profound and encouraging. By following the timeless advice in Greg's books, *Above All Else*, and *The Warrior and The*

Monk, we can happily discover that what we are searching for has been within us the entire time." – *Scott McEwen*, #1 *New York Times* bestselling co-author of *American Sniper*; national bestselling *Sniper Elite* series, and the new *Camp Valor* series of novels

"Greg Amundson's books, *Above All Else*, and *The Warrior and The Monk*, makes experiencing God a little more accessible. They are great primers for the new seeker and wonderful refreshment for the seasoned traveler." – *Rev. Deborah L. Johnson*, Author of *The Sacred Yes* and *Your Deepest Intent*

"Greg Amundson's expert instruction has brought dramatically greater strength, balance, and vital energy into my daily life as it has the lives of countless others. Now, with *The Warrior and The Monk*, Greg guides us in channeling that newfound strength and energy toward a life of service, love, wisdom, and true fulfillment. A powerful and transformational book that will inspire you to live your very best life." – *Girish*, musician, teacher, and author of *Music and Mantras: The Yoga of Mindful Singing for Health, Happiness, Peace and Prosperity*

"Greg Amundson's groundbreaking book, *The Warrior and The Monk*, is an inspiring, timely, and courageously articulated perspective on seeking (and discovering) a personal relationship with God. Greg's newest book, *Above All Else*, is a cherished devotional that I keep with me always. The daily insight he provides into the Word of God is profound." – *Robert Vera*, author of #1 Amazon bestseller, *A Warrior's Faith*, and founder of the Eagle Rise Speakers Bureau

"Greg's books, *Above All Else*, and *The Warrior and The Monk*, capture in words the epic quest we are all on to find happiness, meaning, and fulfillment in life. Greg articulates in a groundbreaking ministry that by turning our attention inward, and seeking God, we can find purpose in our life, and joy through being of service to others." – *Karen Vaughn*, Gold Star mother of US Navy SEAL Aaron Carson Vaughn, and bestselling author of *World Changer: A Mother's Story*

"Greg Amundson IS a Modern Day WARRIOR MONK. Greg has lived it, serving as both an army officer, DEA Special Agent, and SWAT Operator, and in his daily training program to maintain the warrior mind and body that helped create the CrossFit movement of elite tactical fitness. As both a warrior and Christian, I can attest that Greg's books, *Above All Else*, and *The Warrior and The Monk*, bring all these facets of life together and articulates them in a groundbreaking fashion. If you are Christ follower and a man or woman aspiring to live the warrior ethos, I highly recommend Greg's work." – *Jason Redman*, US Navy SEAL (Retired), founder of the Combat Wounded Coalition, and author of *The Trident – The Forging and Reforging of a Navy SEAL Leader*

"Greg is the epitome of the way we all should strive to be better each and every day. With grace, joy and a powerful passion to help others, he instills in all of us the beauty of life and the importance of following God. His books, *Above All Else*, and *The Warrior and The Monk*, will help you along your own path of self-discovery and reveal just how important you are in making this world a better place." – *Kevin R. Briggs*, Sergeant, California Highway Patrol (Retired), and author of *Guardian of the Golden Gate, Protecting the Line Between Hope and Despair*

"Greg Amundson is a warrior with a monk-like mindset. His own self discovery and passion to help others is truly inspiring. Greg empowers us with the tools to a disciplined mind, spirituality, and perfect work-life balance." – *Dr. Suhas Kshirsagar BAMS, MD(Ayu)*, author of #1 Amazon bestseller, *Change Your Schedule Change Your Life*

"Greg's new book, *Above All Else*, is a gem of a tool. I use it in my morning practice to sharpen my soul. The devotionals are short and profound." – *Dr. Gabrielle Lyon*, Co-Founder of The Ash Center for Functional Medicine, and Eagle Rise Speaker

ALSO BY GREG AMUNDSON

Published Books

Your Wife is NOT Your Sister – (And 15 other love lessons I learned the hard way) Robertson Publishing – 2012

Firebreather Fitness – Work Your Body, Mind and Spirit into the Best Shape of Your Life (with TJ Murphy) Velo Press – 2016

The Warrior and The Monk – A Fable About Fulfilling Your Potential and Finding True Happiness. Robertson Publishing – 2018

CrossFit Journal Articles®

A Chink in My Armor

Coaching the Mental Side of CrossFit

CrossFit HQ – 2851 Research Park Drive, Santa Cruz, CA.

Diet Secrets of the Tupperware Man Vol. I

Diet Secrets of the Tupperware Man Vol. II

Forging Elite Leadership

Good Housekeeping Matters

How to Grow a Successful Garage Gym

Training Two Miles to Run 100

ACKNOWLEDGMENTS

First and foremost, I am deeply grateful for the everlasting love and embrace of God and His Son, Jesus Christ. For my beloved parents, Raymond and Julianne Amundson, who encouraged me from a young age to develop my mind, body, and spirit in such a manner that I could be of greater service to others. A great deal of appreciation is extended to Brooklyn Taylor for her brilliant layout and design contributions to this book. I am also indebted to the plank owners of the Patriot Authors Network and Eagle Rise Speakers Bureau: Robert Vera, Josh Mantz, Jay Dobyns, Jason Redman, Kevin Briggs, and Karen Vaughn. Your true "Warrior Monk" spirit continues to inspire me more every day. Finally, to the great mentors and masters whose leadership has deeply influenced my life: Rev. Deborah L. Johnson, Mark Divine, Dan Brulé, Londale Theus, Ken Gray, Chaplain Richard Johnson, Pastor Dave Hicks, Dr. Deepak Chopra, Dr. Suhas Kshirsagar, Raja John Bright, Maharishi Mahesh Yogi, Baba Hari Dass, and Pastor René Schlaepfer.

Above
All Else

DEDICATION

*"Children, obey your parents in everything,
for this pleases the Lord."*
— Colossians 3:20

This book is dedicated in loving memory
to my mom and dad, who provided me with the greatest
example of a "Heart like Christ" I have ever known.

———

*"God is more worthy of your pursuit, attention, and love than all the
other passions of the world combined."*
— Dr. Raymond Amundson

———

"God is entirely devoted to your personal advancement."
— Julianne Amundson

CONTENTS

INTRODUCTION

Faith Of A Child

My father was a man who seemed larger than life. As a child, I believed my dad could *do anything*, and in many respects, his life is a reflection of someone who *did everything*. During the amazing spectrum of my dad's life, he wore the hat of a beach lifeguard, elementary school math teacher, Navy diver, champion bodybuilder and swimmer, martial artist, author, poet, gardener, faithful husband to my mom for over thirty years, Chaplain, and Doctor of Chiropractic. However, my dad's highest calling and greatest focus in life was the role of a minister of God's Word to his family, consisting of my mom, my three younger brothers, and me.

I recall my dad picking me up from Presentation Elementary School one afternoon, at which time I had complained about the strictness of the nuns who were administering my education. My dad comforted me and said, "Your teachers and I want the same thing for you. We want you to put God above everything else in your life. When you put God first, all the other matters of your life will always turn out just right."

These words resonated with my young heart and mind, and ultimately shaped the trajectory and direction of my life. Through Bible study, attending Church, unique life experiences in the military and law enforcement, and, most importantly, the spiritual model of "putting God above all else" provided by my parents, I made an early decision to devote myself to God and His Son, Jesus Christ.

When you devote yourself to God, God devotes Himself to you. This became evident to me as my faith deepened, and God divinely orchestrated events in my life that forced greater dependence on Him, and a more complete understanding of His Word.

Throughout my teenage years and well into my thirties, I had asked God hundreds of times, *"What can I do to cultivate a heart like Jesus Christ?"* The answer arrived one cold and rainy December morning in 2016, as I sat reading the Holy Bible, alone in my condo in Santa Cruz, California. The Scripture seemed to jump off the page as I read it silently several times. Accounting for what is often referred to as the "lost time" of Jesus Christ's life between his twelfth and thirtieth year, the author of the Gospel of Luke, inspired by the Holy Spirit, wrote that "Jesus grew in wisdom, stature, and favor with God and mankind (Luke 2:52).

I sensed that God had confronted me through His Word. A bold voice within my mind seemed to say, "Greg, did you see that verse? Do you understand the awesome implications of what you just read? *Like my Son Jesus Christ, I also want you to increase in wisdom, stature, and favor for all the days of your life.*"

THE WRITING PROCESS: *Listening To God*

Many of my friends and colleagues have been intrigued by the manner in which I integrate and synthesize my writing and lecturing with Scripture, modern principles of self-mastery, leadership, warrior tradition, and positive self-talk. I've been asked hundreds of times, in relation to my books, *Above All Else*, and *The Warrior and The Monk*, in addition to manuscripts for lectures, "How did you write that?" The answer may appear to be overly subjective, but it is the absolute and complete truth: I became silent and still in the presence of God, and allowed His message to flow through me.

Oftentimes, several uninterrupted hours of writing pass by in what seems an instant. Once the connection with God is established, I open my laptop or journal, and allow the Holy Spirit to speak into my mind, then through my fingers, and finally into a written document.

In *Above All Else*, it became clear early in the writing process that God was communicating three general principles:

1. Our thoughts and words are real, and contain manifesting power. We must discipline ourselves to think and speak with a heart like Jesus Christ.

2. What we focus our attention on will increase in our lives. God impressed upon me the importance of praying about, thinking

about, and speaking about what we desire, not the lack of it.

3. Time spent with God is of the utmost importance. Specifically, God wants our focused attention, which can best be expressed to Him through silence and stillness in His presence. It is during this precious time with God that He is able to restore our spirit, improve the quality of our thinking, and rejuvenate our body.

USING THIS BOOK: *Be Strong and Courageous*

In order for you to "increase in wisdom, stature, and favor with God and mankind," you must embrace the truth of God's Word, and honor the temple of your mind, body, and spirit. This book can help you understand God's Word in a powerfully new way, and inspire you to embrace the presence of God more deeply. God calls you to be strong and courageous in His Word, and to set aside time for communion with Him. In order to make the best use of the devotionals contained within these pages, I encourage you to adopt a morning ritual of sacred time alone with God.

Each day, I recommend you follow the five steps outlined below:

1) Upon awakening, remain silent.

2) Move to a place in your home reserved exclusively for meditation and communion with God, and sit silently in His presence. Teaching the principles of prayer, self-mastery, and personal growth, Jesus said, *"When you pray, go into your room and shut the door, and pray to your Father"* (Matthew 6:6).

3) The Psalmist wrote that in order for you to experience peace, transformation, and personal growth, you must first, *"Be still, and know I am God"* (Psalm 46:10). To enter into communion with God, you must make your mind like a still body of water. Close your eyes, and bring awareness to your breathing. Spend several minutes taking long, slow, deep breaths. There is a powerful connection between your breath and your awareness of God's presence. Deep breathing will also help calm the turbulence of your mind, and create a sense of inner peace and tranquility.

4) In the stillness and peace you have cultivated, bring awareness to the very first words you speak. I encourage repeating Bible

verse as your first words. This book contains numerous examples of powerful first-word offerings. As you will discover in the devotionals that follow, your spoken word has manifesting power, and can positively shape your life.

5) Finally, read a page from this book, correlating your reading with the date, while praying that God would *"Open the eyes of your heart, that you would see new and wonderful things in His Word"* (Psalm 119:18). Reflect on the message, Scripture, image, or story, and contemplate how the "wisdom, stature, and favor" gained from God's Word can positively influence your life. Scripture references are numerically notated within the devotionals, and can be referenced in the index section at the end of the book.

BEGIN TODAY

To cultivate a heart and mind like Jesus Christ, and to increase in his likeness, you must develop the absolute certainty that God is with you, and that God is for you. In John 14:12, Jesus said, *"Very truly I tell you, whoever believes in me will do the works I have been doing, and they will do even greater things than these."* There is nothing more exciting, more rewarding, or more worthy of a daily commitment than taking your rightful place, as Jesus did, as a son or daughter of God.

This is the great purpose and mission God desires for you to undertake: *That you would increase in wisdom, stature, and favor for all the days of your life.*

— *Greg Amundson*
Santa Cruz, California, 2018

JANUARY

"Guard, through the Holy Spirit who dwells in us,
the treasure which has been entrusted to you."

— 2 Timothy 1:14

JANUARY 1

*"I can do all things through Christ,
who strengthens me."*

— Philippians 4:13

God is calling you to have a heart like His Son, Jesus Christ. Your birthright as a son or daughter of God is a perfect state of health, radiant wellness, strength, love, resilience, joy, and abundance. The only thing preventing you from abiding within this natural state of divine perfection is your own wrong thinking. Having a heart like Christ requires having a mind like Christ. You are only limited by self-imposed beliefs and ideals. God does not limit you—you limit yourself by immature and undisciplined thinking. When you embrace the presence of God within you, and invite the thoughts of God to take up residence in your mind, the quality of your life will begin to change. As your awareness awakens to the presence of God, your thinking will work for you rather than against you.

JANUARY 2

"Be strong and courageous. For the LORD, your God, will never leave nor forsake you."

— Deuteronomy 31:6

The great illusion of darkness is separation between God and His children. God wants you to understand that He is within you, and you are within Him. God wants to remove the veil of darkness preventing you from seeing and feeling His majestic presence. You tend to feel at the mercy of your life circumstances. When things are going well, you feel close to God. When things are not going well, you feel distant from God. However, God is always the same: He was, is now, and always will be the same. Therefore, your greatest desire should be to know His love and seek His presence. God's presence in your life can be the center-point from which emotions and feelings arise. God is the rock you can safely stand upon, despite the ebb and flow of life's great ocean. When you feel distant from God, it's not God who moved. Return to the peace within you. God is always one breath away from welcoming you home.

JANUARY 3

"Whatever is true, whatever is noble, whatever is right, whatever is pure, whatever is lovely, whatever is admirable – if anything is excellent or praiseworthy – think about such things."

— Philippians 4:8

To develop a heart like Jesus Christ, you must first discipline yourself to think like Christ. By conditioning yourself to seek the good in everything you see, you gradually move the direction of your life towards the good. Similarly, as you begin to elevate and lift the quality of your thoughts towards the good, you will begin to attract conditions, experiences, opportunities, people, attainments, and gifts, which further express your ability to see what is good. Simply put, goodness attracts more of what is good.[1] When a condition does not match the intention of your desires, the error is in your thinking, and nothing else. By changing your thinking and perspective, what you behold and think about will begin to change. Like attracts like. Goodness attracts goodness. Christ-like thinking attracts Christ-like love.

JANUARY 4

"Ask and it will be given to you; seek and you will find; knock and the door will be opened to you."

— Matthew 7:7

As a son or daughter of God, you are blessed with divine manifesting potential. You are a co-creator with God; your birthright is one of infinite creative potential. As Jesus Christ taught through the lesson of his life, you are like a gardener, toiling in the soil of your mind. Your mind and the universal mind of God are one. Therefore, the seeds you plant within your mind will manifest in God's Universe, ultimately becoming the desires of your heart. What you focus your attention on will increase in your life. When you ask for health, you are given health. When you seek love, you will find love. When you knock upon the door of abundance, God will overflow your cup.

JANUARY 5

*"Those who plant seeds of peace will
gather what is right and good."*

— James 3:18

A heart like Jesus Christ awakens when you seek a higher understanding of your God-given, universal creative potential. When you align your thoughts, words, and actions with God, you join Christ in his capacity to heal, love, influence and bless. Uniting with Christ is dependent upon your ability to comprehend the following three rules:

1. What you focus your attention on will increase in your life.

2. Your thoughts and words are the primary vehicles for focusing your attention.

3. You can discipline yourself to use your thoughts and words to accomplish your dreams and goals, and awaken the presence of God within you.

JANUARY 6

"You anoint my head with oil; my cup overflows."

— Psalm 23:5

When you praise God for the desires of your heart, the fulfillment of that desire is magnetized into your life in seemingly miraculous fashion. The testimony of your faith in God is measured before you receive, not afterwards. Jesus Christ taught this in his approach to problems: In one of his most trying acts of faith, Jesus approached the tomb of his dear friend Lazarus, and proclaimed, *"Father, I thank You, for You have heard me."* What could Jesus be thankful for in a time of mourning? Jesus knew he was grateful for the answer to his prayer; that his friend would be restored to life. Jesus therefore called out, *"Lazarus, come forth."* Immediately, Lazarus came out of the tomb, and presented himself to Jesus alive and well.[2] Whatever you desire is within your capacity to achieve, acquire, and hold in hand. Praise God for what you desire, and with positive expectancy, prepare your cup to overflow with God's abundance.

JANUARY 7

"If they obey and serve Him, they shall spend their days in prosperity."

— Job 36:11

Your thoughts about God and Jesus Christ are the most important thoughts within your mind. Therefore, when you think of Jesus Christ, think of a man who was governed by the Word of God; a man who was not easily swayed or tempted; a man who did not deviate from a path he deemed right and just; a leader you could trust absolutely to be true to his convictions; a man who obeyed God; a man completely and utterly united with God. If you desire a heart and mind like Jesus Christ, then you must follow him and strive to become like him. No person can deny that a Christ-like person would inspire confidence and a spirit of fellowship, and may become a shining example of strength and leadership for all the world to see.

JANUARY 8

*"Give and it shall be given to you,
good measure running over."*

— Luke 6:38

Expressing your needs and desires to God through prayer is only the beginning. A heart like Christ means you must learn to give that which you intend for yourself. Once given, the next step is to prepare to receive the response of your good measure. The Prophet Elijah understood this lesson; when three kings came to him and asked him to pray for their victory in battle and rain to supply their soldiers and animals, Elijah applied his divine wisdom. Elijah prayed and gave thanks, then told the kings to return to their camps, dig ditches in the dirt, and prepare for rain. The kings dug, the clouds gathered, the rain fell, and the ditches were filled. The thirst of the soldiers and animals was quenched, and victory was secured.[3] *Whatsoever your desire, believe you have received it, and it shall be yours.*[4]

JANUARY 9

"My God supplies all I need, according to His riches, in the glory of Christ Jesus."

— Philippians 4:19

Everything you attract into your life is ultimately for your good. The habit of your mind is to judge your experiences as either good or bad. You say to yourself, "I desire this," or "I do not desire that." However, when seen from the perspective of God, your need is constantly being supplied, and the supply is always good. God will only bring into your life that which ultimately serves your upward development. If you judge or label any condition in your life as negative, you immediately stop the flow of goodness available to you. On the other hand, when you elevate the quality of your thinking, and seek a Christ-like perspective on the conditions of your life, you allow the power of God to shape all things together for your good.

JANUARY 10

"You do not have, because you do not ask."

— James 4:2

Jesus Christ taught that the faith of a child could access all the riches of God's Kingdom. What then, can you learn from a child? A child abides by God's Law of *"Ask and you shall receive."*[5] A child knows the limitations of their ability to self-provide. When a desire arises outside the child's ability to self-fulfill, they ask their mother or father to provide for them. A child asks for what they specifically desire. A child asks with faith and positive expectancy that their desire, or something even greater, will be fulfilled. A child asks for *what* they desire, not *how* their desire will be supplied. A heart like Christ is dependent upon your ability to embrace the spirit of a child, and bring before the throne of God all your needs. You will have, when you ask.

JANUARY 11

*"And the prayer of faith will save the one who
is sick, and the Lord will raise him up."*

— James 5:15

A heart like Christ requires a daily commitment to abiding in faithful right-thinking. You must learn to think constructively and positively of all persons, all things, all events, and all circumstances. By appraising everything from the highest perspective and Christ-like point of view, your conditions will change as a direct result of your improved thinking. As you discipline yourself to look for the good, you begin to move towards the good, and attract more of which is good into your life. Your perspective is lifted to heavenly realms, with joy, peace, and tranquility gradually becoming the resting point of your mind.

JANUARY 12

*"The tongue has the power of life and death,
and those who love it will eat its fruit."*

— Proverbs 18:21

If you want success, happiness, joy, prosperity, love, health, and fitness, you must exercise and develop the correct use of your thoughts and speech. Whatever you think about and talk about will become the seed you are sowing in the fertile soil of God's Universe. Jesus Christ spoke of light, health, and life, and through the discriminative and disciplined use of his speech, he healed the sick and raised the dead. Jesus taught only light could cast out darkness. Turn the energy of your speech into a source of well-being. Praise God with everything you think, everything you say, and everything you do. *Love the Lord your God with all your heart and with all your soul and with all your mind.*[6]

JANUARY 13

*"Blessed are those who hear the
Word of God and obey it."*

— Luke 11:28

Jesus Christ was an example of a life perfectly aligned with the Word of God. To obey the Word of God necessitates the comprehension of God's Laws. Proper understanding leads to compliance, resulting in a life of harmony, peacefulness, and spiritual fulfillment. One particularly important Spiritual Law to understand and abide by is the Law of Sacrifice. The Law of Sacrifice means to exchange something of lesser for greater value. To obey this Law is to bountifully receive your rightful measure of health, love, success, and happiness. However, oftentimes you unconsciously break this Law, and give up a greater good for a lesser desire. You are sacrificing every day of your life, whether you realize it or not. Therefore, release the lesser energy of negativity, and exchange it for positivity, light, success, prosperity, love, forgiveness, and happiness.

JANUARY 14

*"But small is the gate and narrow the road
that leads to life, and only a few find it."*
— Matthew 7:14

Jesus Christ understood that discipline, self-control, self-mastery, and submission to God, were absolutely necessary to experience both worldly and spiritual success. If you desire to follow Jesus Christ, the first step is a disciplined use of your time, thought and speech. If you intend a life of health, prosperity, purpose and influence, you must fully acknowledge God within you, and embrace the ideals of service, kindness, righteousness, and effective living. The highest example you can follow is the life of Jesus. Throw off laziness, ill thoughts, negativity, disdain, judgment, jealousy, anger, anxiety, and fear for the greater energy of courage, positivity, wellness, abundance, purpose, strength, and tranquility. Focus, concentrate and narrow the road of your thinking to God's Word alone, and the gates of goodness will open before you.

JANUARY 15

*"Do not store up for yourselves treasures on earth.
Instead, store up for yourselves treasure in Heaven."*

— Matthew 6:19

Many years ago, the angel of death appeared before an old man and said,

"Old man, you must now return to the other side."

The old man was afraid to travel alone and replied,

"Can I bring a friend with me?"

The angel said, *"Yes, one friend may accompany you."*

The old man hastily went to his friends: Wealth, Physicality, Strength, Fidelity, Success, and all the other worldly friends he had struggled so long to build up. However, all his worldly friends preferred to remain on earth. Finally the old man approached his friend Good Deeds, and said,

"Spirit, all of my friends have denied me. Will you accompany me to the other side?"

"Yes, dear friend. I will come with you." His friend Good Deeds said.

JANUARY 16

"Let the weak say, 'I am strong.'"

— Joel 3:10

Jesus Christ taught through his life and teachings that rain will fall on the righteous, and the unrighteous. The key difference, however, is the righteous person builds their house upon a foundation of rock. They honor God, and know God is within them. Despite the rain, the righteous person maintains faith that God is strengthening them, providing for them, filling their cup, and correcting their course.[7] The mindset and self-talk for a heart like Christ is, *"I can handle it. I am ready and greater than any storm I face. Almighty God, the Creator of the Universe, is within me, strengthening me. I am equipped, empowered, anointed, and blessed with God's favor. I am strong for God is with me."*

JANUARY 17

"Be still, and know that I Am God."

— Psalm 46:10

God calls for His children to be still and silent in His mighty presence. In stillness, God is able to wash over you with rivers of peacefulness, love, endurance, and restoration. How do you behold the majesty of a sunset, or sunrise? You become still, silent, and physically available to the grandness of what your eyes can see. How do you behold God? You become still, silent, and internally available to Whom your heart can feel. In stillness, you develop sensitivity to *WHO is within YOU*. To develop a heart like Christ, you must give God the gift of your time. When you spend time with God, God spends His time with you.

JANUARY 18

"Behold, the Kingdom of God is within you."

— Luke 17:21

As a child of God, you were born with a hardwired predisposition to search for something that will fulfill you. You instinctively desire a resting point, a foundation, and a sense of completion. You mistakenly believe fulfillment will come from something outside of you, in the form of a human relationship, a career, or a material object. This is why Jesus Christ taught his disciples to be wary of searching, *"Over here, or over there."*[8] You will never satisfy your hunger with anything on the outside, because what you need is already within you. You were made in the image of God. You are a spiritual being. With God, you are whole, magnificent, complete, radiant, divine, and a perfect masterpiece of His eternal beauty.

JANUARY 19

*"Seek first the Kingdom of God, and
everything else will be given to you."*
— Matthew 6:33

God has a master-key for you. Every desire of your heart is made effortlessly available to you, once you have received this key. God's master-key is His promise that when your earnestly seek Him first, then everything you need will be provided for you. This is why Jesus Christ taught his disciples that, *"Every good and great gift comes from the Father."*[9] God is both the Creator and the Source of Creation. When you acknowledge God is within you, and seek him with all your mind, *all your heart and all your strength*, then you will begin to join God in the creative unfolding of your life. You will become an architect in the spiritual realm of manifestation.

JANUARY 20

"My sheep know My voice, and follow wherever I lead."
— John 10:27

There are many voices that compete for your attention. These voices are both within your mind, and from the minds of people in your life. You must develop ears to listen, and eyes to see, the voice of God. Discretion is available when you realize God loves you for WHO you are, not WHAT you do. God's voice is without judgment. God's voice is comforting. God's voice says, *"I believe in you. You can do it."* God's voice is loving and kind. Bring your attention to the *still small voice* within you. Learn to listen to God.

JANUARY 21

"Trust in the Lord God with all your heart,
and lean not on your own understanding."

— Proverbs 3:5-6

One beautiful, warm summer morning, a father took his young son to a grassy field to learn how to fly a kite. As the father took the kite string and handed it to his son, a light breeze filled the air, and effortlessly lifted the kite into the sky.

The young boy smiled grandly as he watched the kite soar against the backdrop of the clouds.

Suddenly, the young boy said,

"Dad, I think the string is holding down my kite."

"Well then son, let go of the string, and see what happens," the father said.

No sooner had the boy released the string, then the kite began to plummet to the ground. Acting quickly, the father and son once again tightly held the string, and the kite began to soar. Sometimes what you think is holding you down, is in fact allowing you to fly.

JANUARY 22

"Whatever you do, do it all for the glory of God."
— 1 Corinthians 10:31

One of the challenges you face is the constructive use of your thinking. When your thoughts are in alignment with the thoughts of God, you effortlessly create happiness for others and yourself. This is why Jesus Christ taught his disciples to *seek first the Kingdom of God*. God's Kingdom is a state of mind, and when you abide in the universal mind of God, you will gain an orderly, disciplined, content, abundant, happy, and peaceful life. Your thoughts are the cause and reason for the conditions in your life. God desires to know and fulfill the desires of your heart. When you entertain heavenly thoughts of health, wellness, prosperity, love, goodwill, and kindness, the effects you desire will manifest in your life.

JANUARY 23

"As a man feels in his heart, so is he."

— Proverbs 23:7

God is within you, and all around you. Can you imagine how God feels? God, the Creator of the Universe, of all that is seen and unseen, feels resounding joy, happiness, love, peacefulness, power, and bliss. These same feelings are your birthright, for God is within you. Take delight in who you are: You are a child of the most high God. The set point of your feelings is a perfect match for the conditions of your life. Therefore, instead of focusing on the conditions, *focus on the cause of the conditions*, which are your thoughts, words, and emotions. You must learn to feel the radiance of God within you. Only then will the conditions of your life rise to the level of heavenly proportion.

JANUARY 24

*"God hears us in whatever we ask. We have
the requests that we have asked of Him."*

— John 5:15

What is your mindset: victor or victim? Do you embrace light or darkness? The most challenging and empowering decision you can make is to take ownership and responsibility for the conditions of your life. Challenging because the conditions may not fully express your heart's desires. Empowering because you have the innate ability to change these conditions, when you change the thoughts and words of your communion with God. God always grants what you ask of Him. Therefore, learn to pray as a victor and with the positive expectancy of a child. Jesus Christ taught that *when you pray, whatever conditions you pray for, believe you have already received them, and they will be yours.*[10] Can you grasp the magnitude of Christ's promise? Do you realize the power you wield through your thoughts and words? Think, speak, and pray about what you desire, not the lack of it. Desire awakens the object of desire, or the absence of it.

JANUARY 25

"Give, and it will be given to you. Good measure, pressed down, shaken together, running over, will be put in your lap."

— Luke 6:38

For anything and everything you desire, you must identify the feeling state of that desire, and in the moment of feeling identification, it will be yours. This is what the Bible verse, *"Give, and it will be given to you"* means. You must give God a message. Conjure up in your heart the feeling of happiness, love, prosperity, goodness, and joy, and you will attract into your life the conditions, experiences, people, and events that are a perfect match to your feeling state. Notice the magnificent promise of God's Word: *"Whatever you so desire will be placed into your lap."* God will glorify your life, for you are His precious child.

JANUARY 26

"Therefore, I tell you, do not worry."
— Matthew 6:25

God is welcoming you home to a place of peacefulness and rest. To develop a heart and mind like Jesus Christ, you must learn to make your mind like a still body of water. The energetic opposite of worry is the feeling of trust. In times of uncertainty, the urgency to "do something" can create self-imposed unease and anxiety. Instead of wasting precious energy on problem solving, restore yourself by becoming still in God's mighty presence. In stillness, you are strong, for you open a channel to the cosmic goodness of God's Kingdom. Think how much more capable a parent is than a child. Even more capable is your God.

JANUARY 27

"Christ in you, the hope of glory."
— Colossians 1:27

Do not mistake the gift for the *giver of the gift*. God is the source of every good gift in your life. The greatest gift God has in store for you is the renewing of your mind. When you become still and silent in the majestic power of God's presence, you are able to receive healing, restoration, and heavenly perspective. In addition to your bountiful receiving, God rejoices in these moments with you. How much does a parent love the joy, happiness, and laughter of their children? Even greater joy can be found within God when you become still in His presence.

JANUARY 28

"Every good gift and every perfect gift is from above, coming down from the father of lights with whom there is no variation or shadow due to change."

— James 1:17

In God's Universe, there is a perfect accounting system. Everything counts. Even the little things count, for many little things make a big thing. During the course of your day, discipline your mind to continually return to the presence of God. Although you may only hold His presence in your mind for a brief moment, these brief moments create momentum and will soon result in sustained awareness of the presence of God. Every time you plant a small seed of love in God's Universe, that seed will result in a harvest of equal or greater measure. Never doubt the power of your thinking to produce the desires of your heart. This is why the Apostle Paul wrote, *"Whatsoever a man sows, that shall he also reap."*[11] By constantly trying to meet and deal with every condition of your life on the better side, you create room for the love of God to flow into your life.

JANUARY 29

"They cried to the LORD in their trouble, and He brought them out of their distresses. He caused the storm to be still, so that the waves of the sea were hushed. Then they were glad because they were quiet, so He guided them to their desired haven."

— Psalm 107:28-30

During times of trouble, you mistake the problem for your *thinking* about the problem. The habit of your mind is to analyze, problem-solve, and internally resist *what already is*. You must understand that it is your thinking about the conditions of your life, not the conditions themselves, which ultimately determine the quality of your experience. Therefore, whenever you witness yourself thinking about a problem, remember God is only one breath away from calming the storm raging in your mind. Become still, and become silent. Allow God into your awareness, and focus your attention upon His *still small voice*. Enjoy the peacefulness and clarity that only God can provide. Once you become still, God will guide your thinking to a heavenly perspective and light the path in front of you.

JANUARY 30

"And we know that for those who love God all things work together for good, for those who are called according to His purpose."

— Romans 8:28

God created you with a unique mission to accomplish during your lifetime. You were designed for a special purpose that only you can do, and until you are expressing the unique talents and abilities within the fabric of your being that God specifically created, a *still small voice* in your heart will whisper gentle reminders of your true purpose. Ask God to illuminate within your mind the great adventure He wants you to pursue. When you shine the light of your life, all of Heaven rejoices over you.

JANUARY 31

*"'For I know the plans I have for you,' declares
the Lord, 'Plans for welfare and not for evil,
to give you a future and a hope.'"*

— Proverbs 16:9

Everything you have experienced in life has been carefully choreographed by God for your greater good. Through God's perfect plan, this exact moment in your life has divinely unfolded according to His glory. You are safe, you are protected, and *the forces that are for you are greater than the forces that are against you.*[12] God has great plans, opportunities, appointments, prosperity, love, adventure, and service in store for you. Remain positive in your mind, holding strong to the anchor of God's promise.

FEBRUARY

"So that Christ may dwell in your hearts through faith. And I pray that you, being rooted and established in love, may have power, together with all the Lord's holy people, to grasp how wide and long and high and deep is the love of Christ."

— Ephesians 3:17-18

FEBRUARY 1

*"The harvest is truly plenteous,
but the laborers are few."*

— Matthew 9:37

The exertion of willpower in your life is not the denial of happiness, but rather turning the attention from temporary and fleeting pleasures to the eternal Kingdom of God. You must learn to identify the permanent treasures God has in store for you, and then focus all of your willpower on their multiplying. This is what Jesus Christ meant when he taught the disciples to build their everlasting treasures in Heaven, as opposed to the treasures of earth, which *moth and rust would corrupt and where thieves break through and steal away*.[13] What is everlasting? Goodwill, kindness, love, forgiveness, service, devotion, prayer, and faithfulness. These are eternal treasures the cosmic karmic bank invests with interest into your soul-account.

FEBRUARY 2

---

*"The peace of God, which surpasses all understanding,
will guard your hearts and your minds in Christ Jesus."*

— Philippians 4:6

God longs to envelop you with peacefulness. All too often, the storm in your mind is the cause of your restlessness, unease, fear, and worry. As one nail can drive out another, one good thought rooted in the Word of God can drive out darkness and replace it with light. Jesus Christ taught that only light could cast out darkness. Instead of tossing about the vast sea of anxiousness, or trudging through the shadows of negativity, become still in the presence of God, allowing His light to fill your mind, body, and spirit. When your mind becomes like a still body of water, you are able to see the world through the eyes of Christ.

FEBRUARY 3

"Whoever believes in me, as Scripture has said,
rivers of living water will flow through them."

— John 7:38

A river gathers a little bit of everything that flows through it. When the greatness of God flows through you, His Spirit becomes part of you forevermore. The deepest part of the river is where the water moves the slowest. When you become still in the presence of God, your mind takes on the qualities of a deep and slow moving body of water. Spend time in this stillness, allowing God to permeate your mind and elevate the quality of your thinking. God asks His children to *"be still, and know."*[14] There is a part of you that is always still. There is a part of you that always knows. When you come to rest in the stillness and knowingness of God, you will happily discover the river of God has been running through you the entire time.

FEBRUARY 4

---

*"The LORD will fight for you, and
you have only to be still."*

— Exodus 14:14

The world tends to elicit a downward gravitational pull on your thinking. When you spend too much time immersed in worldly concerns, your thinking becomes stagnant, dark, and dull. God longs to spiral your thinking upward into heavenly realms. When you spend time with God, His radiant presence restores your mind and calms your restless spirit. *He will elevate the quality of your thinking and put a new and right spirit within you.*[15] Into the stillness of your mind, God is able to drop seeds of inspiration that radiate positively throughout every corner of your life.

FEBRUARY 5

"Today is the day the LORD has made.
Let us rejoice and be glad in it."

— Psalm 118:24

You must come to understand and appreciate that your thinking will influence the way you see your environment. When you change the way you think about something, what you think about begins to change. Your ability to reflect upon and consciously choose your thoughts is a marvelous gift from God, and often underutilized by His children. The first step is to witness the quality of your thinking. Then, gently begin to align your thoughts with the Word of God. Your ability to understand and rejoice that God *is within you* will increase when your thinking shifts from the world to His presence. God is available to you this very moment. He longs to make contact with you, but His presence cannot be revealed when your mind has regressed to the past or projected itself into the future. Therefore, you must discipline yourself to continually realign your awareness to the present moment. As the Psalmist wrote, *"Today is the day the Lord has made."*

FEBRUARY 6

"Call to me and I will answer you and tell you great and unsearchable things you do not know."

— Jeremiah 33:3

There is a small space between everything that happens to you, and your reaction to it. In this space is the peace of God. With practice, you can learn to instantly discern the perfect response to every situation. As you become still in the presence of God, then His presence within you will begin to expand. You will notice His influence on your thinking in critical moments. The stillness you cultivate through meditation on His presence will carryover into your daily life experience. As the Psalmist wrote, *"Goodness and love will surely follow you all the days of your life."*[16]

FEBRUARY 7

"Consider it pure joy, my brothers and sisters, whenever you face trials of many kinds, because you know that the testing of your faith produces perseverance."

— James 1:2-3

A wealthy man hired a builder to design and construct a home for his family. The wealthy man detailed his expectations for the home to include beauty, robustness, strength, safety, and peacefulness. The builder concluded the only suitable wood to construct such a home must come from the north side of the mountain.

The builder explained to the wealthy man, *"I recommend only using timber from the north side of the mountain."*

"Why must we use that wood?" inquired the wealthy man.

"The rigors of Mother Nature on the north side of the mountain are harsh. The snow is deeper, and the cold is colder. The winds are stiffer, and the sun is rarely seen. The harshness of the weather contributes to a timber that is unparalleled in strength, refinement, and beauty," explained the builder.

FEBRUARY 8

"So Jesus said, 'If you abide in my Word, you are truly my disciples, and you will know the truth, and the truth will set you free.'"

— John 8:31-32

God is calling you to be His disciple. He is beckoning you to embrace your spiritual center, and to have a heart like His Son, Jesus Christ. To become a *disciple* of God means to *discipline* yourself to live according to God's Word. Thinking positively is not a luxury or idle pastime. Your mind was designed to communicate with Christ. However, you must first learn the language with which Christ wants to communicate with you. Christ taught his disciples to think in a way that was harmonious, lovely, gracious, kind, courageous and pure. When the vibration of your mind and thoughts are positive, you join Christ in a heavenly realm of intimacy and divine union.

FEBRUARY 9

*"I am the vine; you are the branches. If you remain
in me and I in you, you will bear much fruit."*

— John 15:5

Jesus Christ knew he was the Son of God, and with the authority of a mighty Prince of Peace, he performed miracles on earth through the power of his Father. Christ was desirous to inspire all who believed in him to embrace God as their Heavenly Father, and true source of supply. Your ability to live as a conduit of God's love is dependent upon the quality of your thinking. The good within the conditions of your life will always be in direct proportion to the good thoughts within the temple of your mind. When you welcome the embrace of God, you surrender into His loving arms the self-imposed limitations of negativity, poverty, lack, and fear. Calmness, justice, faith, courage, prosperity, and kindness—these are but a few of the glorious seeds God planted in your soul at birth. When you dutifully nourish these seeds, then the *fruit of the vine* will bless every corner of your life.

FEBRUARY 10

"Delight yourself in the LORD, and He will give you the desires of your heart."

— Psalm 37:4

Whatever you desire to be, you may become now—in this very moment. Non-accomplishment, poverty, idleness, anxiety, and lack are a result of your perpetual postponement. However, having the ability to postpone, you also inherently have the ability to accomplish and acquire. When you realize this truth, you will have the ability today to become your ideal self. This is why Jesus Christ taught his disciples, *"When you pray, whatever you pray for, believe that you already have it, and it shall be yours."*[17] Discipline yourself to listen and obey the words of Jesus Christ, and the commands of your Heavenly Father. Nurture the seeds of faith, courage, optimism, and positive expectancy that reside in the fertile soil of your mind.

FEBRUARY 11

"Prepare for your work outside; get everything ready for yourself in the field, and after that build your house."
— Proverbs 24:27

Whatever you can see and believe in your mind, you can accomplish. The most important work is always the task of expanding your awareness to the infinite creative power of God within you. There is no difficulty that will not yield before you, and no object of your desire that will not speedily be actualized, when you align your thinking with God.[18] God is both the *creation* and *source of creation*.[19] Whatever you desire in your heart will be yours, when you can both see and feel yourself as having already acquired it. Therefore, the steps to actualizing your dreams and desires will always be as follows:

1. Pray.

2. Believe.

3. Receive.

FEBRUARY 12

---

*"For which of you, desiring to build a tower,
does not first sit down and count the cost,
whether he has enough to complete it?"*

— Luke 14:28

Jesus Christ taught that you would reap the results of your own thoughts, words, and actions. Therefore, you must learn to begin right each morning by connecting with God and aligning your thoughts with His Word. Your desire to be happy, prosperous, and of service to the world is contingent upon the quality and grandness of your thinking. The set-point of your mind and feelings will surely come to pass in your life. Discipline yourself to think continually upon that which is *pure, happy, kind, right, lovely, just, and beautiful.*[20]

FEBRUARY 13

"Enlarge the place of your tent, and let the curtains of your habitations be stretched out; do not hold back; lengthen your cords and strengthen your stakes."

— Isaiah 54:2

Your must discipline yourself to think exclusively of what you desire, not the absence of it. This principle of God's Law of Attraction is enough to change your life forevermore. For example, if you were cold, you would not work with cold in order to get warm. You would build a fire, draw near to it, and enjoy the warmth of the flames from the fire. As the heat from the fire gradually warmed you, then the cold would disappear, for cold is the absence of heat. This principle works with equal precision in your mind: Think about what you desire, and the lack of it will surely disappear from your life. Think about health, purity, loveliness, kindness, prosperity, and peacefulness. God's intention for you *is for goodness all the days of your life.*[21]

FEBRUARY 14

"The point is this: Whoever sows sparingly will also reap sparingly, and whoever sows bountifully will also reap bountifully."
— 2 Corinthians 9:6

Whatever you think in your mind will grow in your life. This is what Jesus Christ meant when he taught the disciples the principle of, *"reaping what you sow."* The good gardener goes out into their garden, and works tediously to pull out every weed. If some condition is challenging you, focus on the *cause of the condition*, which is a weed within the temple of your mind. It is important for you to understand a condition is the *effect that you see*; it is not the *actual cause*. Weed out the cause and replace it with the right kind of thinking. Fear must be replaced by thoughts of courage. Lack must be replaced by thoughts of plenty. Sickness must be replaced by thoughts of health. Separateness from anything you desire must be replaced by thoughts of God.

FEBRUARY 15

"Pray continually."

— Thessalonians 5:17

Jesus Christ taught his disciples, *"Seek first the Kingdom of God, and everything else will be added to you."*[22] Heaven is a state of mind, and is available for you to experience in this very moment. To enter into God's Kingdom, you must first align your thinking with the mind of God. To gain intimacy with God and the desires of your heart, you must discipline yourself to maintain a positive, constructive and orderly state of thinking. Whatever dominant thought you hold in your mind, whether you desire it or not, according to God's Law of Attraction, will grow and increase in your life. Therefore, *pray continually*, and remain in a constant state of awareness of the presence of God within you.

FEBRUARY 16

"Continue steadfastly in prayer, being watchful in it with thanksgiving."

— Colossians 4:2

The hierarchy to entering the Kingdom of God is the following: Thoughts. Words. Actions. Habits. Character. Destiny. Therefore, you hold the key to the gates of Heaven in your mind. Thinking determines the conditions of your life, and to have better conditions, you must have better thoughts. The greatest thoughts to hold in your mind are of God, the Son, and the Holy Spirit.

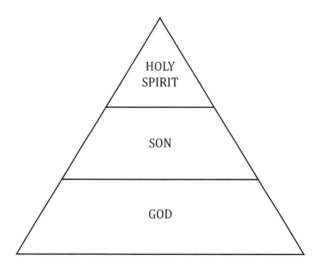

FEBRUARY 17

"For God so loved the world, that He gave His only Son, that whoever believes in him should not perish but have eternal life."

— John 3:16

You will discover the positive mental attitude of the person who thinks, *"I Can"* (in contrast with another person who thinks, *"I Can't"*) is oftentimes the only difference between who succeeds and who fails. Therefore, you must direct all your mental energy towards the development of personal belief and faith in God. Any endeavor or challenge, regardless how trivial or grand in nature, is never yours alone, for *with God all things are possible.*[23] Allow your internal compass to guide you to a life of happiness and success by continually realigning your thinking with this Truth: *Through Christ, you can do all things.*[24]

FEBRUARY 18

*"Jesus said to him, 'Have you believed
because you have seen me? Blessed are those
who have not seen and yet have believed.'"*
— John 20:29

What you can see and believe in your mind, you can have in hand. If you wish to change your circumstances, then you must start by changing your thoughts. Since you alone are responsible for your thoughts, you are also responsible for your circumstances. Every thought you think and every word you speak creates according to its own kind. God's Law of Attraction, actualized though your spoken word, is always working and demonstrating its power according to the thoughts you habitually entertain. Therefore, begin today to think only thoughts that will bring you health and happiness. Repeat the Word of God with deep concentration until you establish a new and positive habit of thought. When it becomes as natural for you to think of God as it does to breathe, then you will truly know His grace and mercy.

FEBRUARY 19

"For with the heart one believes and is justified, and with the mouth one confesses and is saved."

— Romans 10: 9-10

The desires of your heart must match the confessions of your mouth. *The greatest ship is turned about in a mighty sea by the use of a small rudder.*[25] Develop the discipline to speak only with positive expectancy, optimism, and personal belief. It is far better to remain in silence than defeat yourself with negativity. Vow to trust in God's love and grand plan for your life. You are a child of God and are destined for happiness, success, prosperity, love, service, peacefulness, and joy. *Surely goodness and love will follow you all the days of your life.*[26]

FEBRUARY 20

---

*"Therefore, put on the full armor of God,
so that when the day of evil comes, you
may be able to stand your ground."*

— Ephesians 6:11

You are protected and surrounded by an army of Angels. *The forces that are for you are always greater than the forces that are against you.*[27] No challenge, opposition, enemy, or setback could possibly defeat you, for you are a child of God. Therefore, approach problems with a gentle touch, and sense of peaceful security. God is with you, God is for you, and God is within you. *God is fighting your battles for you.*[28] Any form of worry is a lack of trust in the great plan and adventure God has in store for you. With the courage of ten thousand mighty warriors, proceed confidently into this day, radiantly shining the light of Jesus Christ through your words, and by your actions.

FEBRUARY 21

"Work willingly at whatever you do, as though you were working for the Lord God rather than for people."

— Colossians 3:23

God created you to accomplish great things in life. When you are in perfect alignment with God, inspiration, divine guidance, and creativity will become a natural state of being for you. Therefore, whatever you do, perform it as both an offering to God and to the world. When your daily tasks take on the quality of a gift, you are doubly blessed. Once for the extension of love that your gift provides to others. Twice because you will surely reap the return of the gift you give away.

FEBRUARY 22

"The blessing of the LORD makes rich."
— Proverbs 10:22

You have a tendency to accomplish things through your own effort. There is another way. If a wave suddenly discovered that it was really the ocean, it would see the ocean had temporarily become its small self, and many other waves as well.[29] Therefore, perform every activity with the thought of God within the temple of your mind. Welcome God into your life, and He will come to you and you will realize that He is the Ocean of Life, and that you are a tiny wave, and that you are one with the Ocean. The moments you are in harmony with God and abide in His holy presence, you instantly become available to the blessings He has stored up for you. *A table will be prepared before you, your cup of abundance will overflow, countless riches will eagerly await your receipt, and goodness will account for all the days of your life.*[30] Let go. Let God.

FEBRUARY 23

"Take the helmet of salvation and the sword of the Spirit, which is the Word of God."

— Ephesians 6:17

There is a mighty power in your words. Creative energy resonates throughout God's Universe every time you speak. Therefore, *guard your tongue*, disciplining yourself to honor the great teaching of Jesus Christ: *Ask and you shall receive.*[31] Every word you speak into the fertile soil of universal potentiality produces an *effect* in your life.[32] Ensure the seeds you plant are rich in light, love, kindness, abundance, health, and positivity. Let the Word of God work through you. This is the best part of your daily devotion. When God is walking through your feet, working through your hands, and speaking through your voice, then you will know God, and He will know you. Remember at all times that you are a child of God, and are one with His presence. When you remember and know that truth, *all things will be added to you.*

FEBRUARY 24

"Look to the LORD and His strength;
seek His face always."

— Chronicles 6:11

Stillness and trust are two sides of the same coin. In stillness, you display courageous trust in God, and His ability to provide *all your needs*. Similarly, you testify trust in God by becoming still in moments of decision, allowing the Spirit of God to elevate the quality of your thinking. Stillness in God's presence will develop trust. By trusting God, you will become still.

FEBRUARY 25

"I will praise you LORD my God, with all my heart. I will glorify your Name forever."

— Psalm 86:12

Jesus Christ understood the mighty power of praise and stillness. Following a long day of walking and worship, five thousand people stood before Christ, all of them hungry.

"How will we feed all these people?" the disciples asked Jesus.

Trusting in his Father's ability to provide all their needs, Jesus told the five thousand to sit down, and become still.

Jesus then praised God for what he had in hand—the meager five loaves of bread and two fish. Christ knew in order to attract abundance for himself and others, the first step was gratefulness and praise, thus opening the channel for God's love.

Jesus received God's love, and fed the five thousand.

Be still.

Be grateful.

Praise God.

Receive His love.

FEBRUARY 26

"The LORD shall satisfy your desire with good things."
— Psalm 103:5

God is the source of supply for everything your heart desires. Therefore, in the creative process, *believing always precedes* seeing. Concepts of lack, limitation, and poverty are an illusion of your mind. In God's Universe there is only infinite abundance. You must embrace your birthright as a creator, and join God in the creative process, which is His intention for you. You were made in the image of God, and are therefore both a creation and a creator. Your practice is to focus on *what you desire*. God will provide the means. When the desires of your heart are formed and held clearly in your mind, God will always provide for the fulfillment of your intention, or something even greater. *Your God supplies all your needs, according to His riches, in the Glory of Christ Jesus.*[33]

FEBRUARY 27

*"A man can receive nothing, unless it
has been given him from Heaven."*

— John 3:27

Everything you desire in this moment exists as formless energy in God's Universe. Because God is the source of your supply, and God is infinite in His ability to provide, you must condition your mind to resonate with abundance. This is accomplished in three ways:

1. *Seek first the Kingdom of God.*

2. Focus on what you desire, not the lack of it.

3. Praise God for his ability to *provide all your needs.*

When your thoughts, words, emotions and actions are in harmony with God, the desires of your heart will be effortlessly placed at your feet. *Seek first God's Kingdom and His righteousness, and everything else will be given to you.*[34]

FEBRUARY 28

"Stand firm, hold your position, and see the salvation of the LORD on your behalf."

— 2 Chronicles 2:17

You must learn to bring awareness to both the quality and quantity of your thinking. The first step in developing sensitivity to your thinking is to become still in the presence of God. This is what the Psalmist meant when he wrote: *"Be still, and know."* When you sit silently in the presence of God, the turbulence of your mind will begin to subside. In silence, your mind will take on the qualities of a pristinely still body of water. From the surface of the water, the *still small voice of God* will sink into the depths of your heart.[35] Peace will envelop you, and a blanket of divine protection will be laid over your mind.

FEBRUARY 29

"Do you know that your body is a temple of the Holy Spirit within you, which you have from God?"

— 1 Corinthians 6:19

Where awareness goes, energy flows. To develop a heart like Jesus Christ, you must continually bring your awareness to the presence of God in you. Increased awareness of God can be accomplished by closing your eyes, and turning your attention inward. Take a deep breath in through your nose, and a slow breath out through your mouth. God will reveal Himself to you by feelings of comfort, peacefulness, and tranquility. When you feel distant from God, it was not God who moved. God is always within you. God is always for you. God is always with you. His holy presence is always just one breath away.

MARCH

"To whom God willed to make known what is the riches of the glory of this mystery among the Gentiles, which is Christ in you, the hope of glory."

— Colossians 1:27

MARCH 1

"If we confess our sins, he is faithful and just to forgive us our sins and to cleanse us from all unrighteousness."

— 1 John 1:9

Jesus Christ taught that the originating place of every action was within the mind. If lust, or greed, or revenge, or rage was committed in the mind, there was a sin, even if an overt act was never committed. This is what Christ meant when he said, *"For out of the heart of man, proceed evil thoughts, adulteries, murders, thefts, and foolishness."*[36] Fortunately, Christ also taught a method for removing thought producing sin from your mind. Forgiveness is the means to liberate your mind from all forms of negativity, and the first requirement for uprooting sinful thoughts. Once negativity has been removed, the next step is to plant in the fertile soil of your mind thoughts of goodness, kindness, peacefulness, abundance, health and wellness. The master thought to hold in your mind is of God, the Son, and the Holy Spirit.

MARCH 2

"For it is with your heart that you believe and are justified, and it is with your mouth that you profess your faith and are saved."
— Romans 10:10

God wants to restore your mind. As the quality of your thinking improves, so will your words. Your improved thinking and speaking will lead to right actions, habits, and the development of Christ-like character. Your character will determine your destiny.

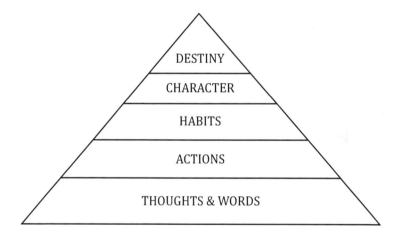

MARCH 3

*"Before they call I will answer; while
they are yet speaking I will hear."*
— Isaiah 65:24

Nothing can separate you from God's loving embrace. Many worldly relationships are based on the principle of *cause and effect*. However, God's love for you transcends reason and human understanding. *Nothing you do, or fail to do, will affect God's love for you*. God loves you for the person you were yesterday, the person you are today, and the person you will be tomorrow. His love is unconditional, everlasting, and eternal. Rest easy in God's love, and take comfort in relinquishing the need to perform. Spend less time *doing* and more time *being a child of God*.

MARCH 4

*"Do not be afraid; the LORD your God
himself will fight for you."*

— Deuteronomy 3:22

God wants to help you navigate through this day. He wants to lead you along glorious paths, and protect you from dangerous pitfalls along the way. Your mission is to stay alert to His mighty presence, and to keep your eyes fixed on Him. Instead of worrying what today holds, or what tasks must be completed, focus on drawing close to God. Choose to lean on God, trusting that everything before you today will be for your good. God is with you. God is for you. *God is fighting your battles for you.*

MARCH 5

"I have fought the good fight, I have finished the course, I have kept the faith."

— 2 Timothy 4:7

Two boys dove into a river early one morning, challenging each other to swim across the vast body of water. They swam with strength and endurance, and the lead swimmer, always looking forward, continued swimming toward the sun, rising above the other shore. When he reached his destination at the far shore, he looked back and noted his friend was standing across the river, where they originally started.

When he met his friend later in the day, he asked him, *"Why did you turn back?"*

The timid swimmer replied, *"When I got halfway across, I looked back and saw how far I had come and was afraid I could not make it, so I turned back. How were you able to swim across?"*

The boy said, *"I kept my eyes on the rising sun, and kept moving toward the light."*

MARCH 6

"One gives freely, yet grows all the richer; another withholds what he should give, and only suffers want. Whoever brings blessings will be enriched, and one who waters will himself be watered."

— Proverbs 11:24-25

God is able to do more and provide more than you could ever ask or imagine. As you continue to elevate the quality of your prayers and petitions, God is able to elevate the quality of His blessings into your life. Therefore, your daily practice is to experience life through the mind of Jesus Christ, rather than your own limited understanding and capacity. God is continually at work in your life. God is at all places at all times. *He is within you, around you, and on the path slightly ahead of you.*[37] You are taking in life one experience at a time. However, God has your big picture in mind, and is continually bringing you one step closer to your prayers and requests. The great secret to receiving your heartfelt prayers is to continually thank God for their receipt, trusting that in His perfect time, *you will receive immeasurably more than you can imagine.*[38]

MARCH 7

"Abraham believed God, and it was counted to him as righteousness, and he was called a friend of God."

— James 2:23

The original North American Indian language was rich with meaning, and eloquent in its sophistication. For example, the translation for the word "friend" was *"one who carries my sorrows on his back."* God, the Creator of the Universe, of all that is both seen and unseen, wants to be your friend. God longs to carry your burdens, your sorrows, and your challenges. Instead of struggling under your own strength, rest in the peaceful presence of God. Allow God to elevate the quality of your thinking, and to help you navigate this day. *You can do all things through Christ who is strengthening you.*[39]

MARCH 8

"But I say onto you, that you resist not evil."
— Matthew 5:39

Water is very powerful, and is a perfect example of Jesus Christ's teaching of non-resistance. You can see where water has worn away the hardest rock, and how it sweeps away everything before it. Trees, buildings, bridges – nothing can withstand its force. Yet, note how the great river begins; as a tiny, innocent stream. When the little stream reaches a boulder, it does not stop at the foot of the obstacle and wait for its force to build up. Instead, the little stream weaves around the obstacle, for its primary intention is reaching a larger stream, then a river, and finally the mighty ocean. Similarly, allow your energy and momentum to carry you towards God. When you move closer to God, God moves closer to you.

MARCH 9

"Let your eyes look directly forward,
and your gaze be straight before you."

— Proverbs 4:27

God wants to be part of every aspect of your life. Bring every conceivable detail before Him, and resist the temptation to do things on your own. Ask God to help you discern where to focus your energy and life force. You have a special purpose to fulfill in life, and in order to succeed, you must the ensure wise and disciplined use of your time. *Keep your eyes focused on the path directly in front of you.*

MARCH 10

*"Create in me a clean heart, Oh God,
and renew a right spirit within me."*

— Psalm 51:10

You must set aside time each day to be Holy in God's presence. To be "Holy" means to be *set aside for sacred use.* When you become still and silent before God, He begins to transform your mind, body and heart. You are renewed, lifted up, and restored. *You are lifted up on the wings of an eagle.*[40] In the same manner you are able to absorb the healing benefits of sunshine, your soul soaks in the glorious Light of God, which then radiates through you into the entire world.

MARCH 11

"My presence will go with you, and I will give you rest."
— Exodus 33:14

God is in the silence between your thoughts. God is in the space between your breaths. God is in the stillness between the beatings of your heart. Every moment of every day, God is for you and God is with you. Even in the moments when you feel distant from God, His nearness to you is like a shadow, hovering over your shoulder. God is with you now, and will be with you for eternity.

MARCH 12

*"You will seek me and find me, when
you seek me with all your heart."*

— Jeremiah 29:13

You live in a word full of constantly changing circumstances, stimuli and events. By focusing on what is always changing, you become easily distracted, weary and anxious. Therefore, direct all of your senses to what never changes. Become still in the presence of the One who is the same *yesterday, today, and forever more.*[41]

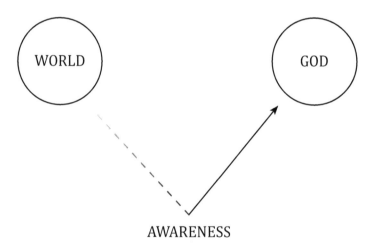

WORLD

GOD

AWARENESS

MARCH 13

*"Behold I am with you, and will
keep you wherever you go."*

— Genesis 28:15

Your attention holds your awareness. Wherever your attention is, your awareness will be there as well. Your attention, which is your concentrated awareness, breaths life into whatever it rests upon. When you focus your attention on something, you increase its power in your life. When you take your attention away from something, it fades out of your life. Hence the power of prayer, and the disciplined bringing of your attention to the presence of God. There is a momentum that is generated when you begin your day in silence and prayer. This mighty force is carried with you throughout the day, paving a path before you with goodness. Return your attention to God, and He will return His attention to you.

MARCH 14

---

*"Jesus Christ is the same yesterday
and today and forever."*

— Hebrews 13:8

Jesus Christ taught his disciples that eternal life could be found through him alone. As you identify more fully with God, you will begin to discern what retains permanence throughout eternity, and what is simply a temporal cloud passing though the sky of your awareness. As clouds come and clouds go, observe them without attachment. Learn to appreciate the rhythm of life, which is evident in nature all around you. Seasons come and go. Thoughts come and go. Emotions come and go. People come and go. God is forever.

MARCH 15

"The tongue has the power of life and death, and those who love it will eat it's fruit."

— Proverbs 18:21

Your capacity to speak affords you with the same creative power God used to form the world out of nothing. Therefore, you must learn to exercise discernment before opening your mouth. In the silence of your heart, ask yourself if what you intend to say will bring peace, love, and happiness to you and others. By spending time alone with God, you will develop skillfulness in your speech, and your words will be of great comfort to everyone who hears them. Remember at all times the power of the spoken word, and that whatever you speak about will receive its mighty creative force. Speak of love. Speak of life. Speak of God.

MARCH 16

"Therefore, if anyone is in Christ, the new creation has come: The old has passed away, the new is here!"

— 2 Corinthians 5:17

One morning an old wise man was relaxing on his back in the middle of a pristine, grassy field. Completely at peace, the old man looked up to the Heavens with contentment.

A young boy happened upon the man and asked,

"Old man, what are you doing?"

The old man replied, *"I am laying here watching my thoughts pass by."*

The young boy said, *"It looks like you are watching clouds pass by."*

"Young boy, it is the same thing," answered the old man.

MARCH 17

"In the beginning was the Word, and the Word was with God, and the Word was God."

— John 1:1

"Word" means intelligent vibration and intelligent energy coming forth from God. As the Apostle John wrote in the Bible, the Word in the beginning was the source of all created cosmic substances in God's Universe. Similarly, because the presence of God is within you, when you speak your words are formed of sound energy and vibration, and through the power of the Holy Spirit, everything you say is imbued with intelligent meaning. Your words are like seeds that are planted in a fertile soil of unlimited creative potential. You are a manifesting human spirit capable of creating peace, love, abundance, happiness, and goodness. Speak with the authority of God within you.

MARCH 18

"But as many received him, to them he gave power to become the sons of God, even to them that believe on his name."

— 1 John 12-13

God's light shines equally on all His children. However, because of delusive ignorance and false belief in separateness, not all of God's children receive and reflect His love alike. Sunlight falls on both a lump of coal and a diamond, but only the diamond is able to absorb and reflect the light in brilliant beauty.[42] The carbon in the coal has within it the ability to become a diamond. All the coal requires is the consciousness and awareness of its great potential. To become a Child of God is not something to acquire or work towards. Rather, all you must do is receive God's light and realize that the presence of God is always with you. You were born blessed. You were born full of favor and prosperity. You were born with everything you need to accomplish your dreams and goals. You were born a divine child of God.

MARCH 19

"For you have been taught by God to love one another."

— 1 Thessalonians 4:9

The Wind and Sun once had a quarrel. The Wind boasted that he was much stronger than the Sun.

The Wind said, *"See that old man with the big coat on? I bet I can make him take off his coat quicker than you can."*

"All right, let's see," said the Sun.

The Sun then went and hid behind a cloud. The Wind blew and blew, causing a horrible storm. However, the harder the Wind blew, the tighter the old man wrapped his coat around him.

Then it was the Sun's turn. She came out from behind the clouds, and smiled with great warmth upon the old man. Soon, the old man began to smile, and he remarked,

"What a beautiful afternoon it has become."

The old man then took off his coat and began to enjoy the day.

MARCH 20

"We have fled to God for refuge to lay hold upon the hope set before us, which hope we have as an anchor of the soul, both sure and steadfast."
— Hebrews 6:18-19

You must learn to develop hope in God. To hope in God with all your heart, all your soul, and all your mind is a cardinal virtue and testimony of your faith. The original meaning of "hope" was, *"the application of our faith that makes us firm and resolute, the understanding that drives us to endure seemingly impossible challenges."* Allow God to be the anchor of your soul. Stand strongly in the certainty of God's enduring love for you.

MARCH 21

"The LORD says, 'Though the mountains be shaken and the hills be removed, yet my unfailing love for you will not be shaken, nor my covenant of peace be removed.'"

— Isaiah 54:10

When it rains heavily, the water does not necessarily penetrate the surface of the earth. If the surface is dry, compressed and hard, the rainwater will temporarily flood the surface, then run off. With the surface water gone, the earth is barren and hard once again. However, if the rain continues for several days, and the water remains on the surface for an extended period of time, the water will begin to seep deep into the soil, allowing for life and growth to take place.[43] This analogy helps illustrate the manner in which God's Word acts on your heart. When you continue to spend reading and meditating on the Word of God, His grace, mercy and peace will begin to seep deeply into your entire being. The outer conditions of your life will soon reflect the inner conditions of your mind. *Come near to God and He will come near to you.*[44]

MARCH 22

"The LORD your God loves you."
— Deuteronomy 23:5

God loves you. God is with you. *God takes great delight in you, and rejoices over you with singing.*[45] During the course of your day, discipline yourself to take moments of silence and solitude to feel the presence of God's love. These brief moments will become a refuge, and provide much needed nourishment for your mind and soul. In silence and solitude, it will be much easier for your seeking heart to receive His splendor. Therefore, approach God often during the adventures that await you today.

MARCH 23

"As a man thinks in his heart, so is he."

— Proverbs 23:7

The thoughts, feelings, and emotions you energize will attract circumstances, events, people, and ultimately an entire reality that will perfectly match your energetic set point. This is why the Prophet's wrote that whatever you *feel in your heart you will become*. In the Bible, the word "heart" was used in a very special way, and often referred to our modern understanding of the subconscious mind. Therefore, the Bible teaches the principle that *your thoughts become things*. One of the best ways to establish thoughts and conditions of peacefulness, love, contentment, and abundance is to spend time alone with God. Turn your attention inward, close your eyes, and become still. Gradually, the turmoil of your mind will become calm, and God's love will tenderly envelop you. *Seek first the Kingdom of God, and everything else will be added to you.*[46]

MARCH 24

"Let the peace of Christ rule in your hearts,
since as members of one body you were
called to peace. And be thankful."
— Colossians 3:15

God is speaking to you from the depths of eternity. In order to hear *His still small voice*, you must learn to contact the depths of your being, where God has taken up residence. God is alive and well within you. In order to tune into His presence, you must become still and silent, allowing the energetic vibration of God to radiate throughout your entire being. Spending time with God is like priming the pump of a well. At first, your willpower is needed to become still and silent in His presence. However, as you continue to bring God the sacrifice of your time, His spirit is able to expand within you. Your direct experience of God's grace and mercy will produce deeper levels of communion, until you are overflowing with God's love. God is holding nothing back from you. Therefore, hold nothing back from God.

MARCH 25

"We walk by faith, and not by sight."
— 2 Corinthians 5:7

There is an open road ahead of you, leading to the Kingdom of God. Along the way, Jesus Christ is your traveling companion, and he is eager to help you navigate the twists, turns, peaks, and valleys of your journey. Your challenge is to stop focusing on your problems and limitations, and to instead focus on God. To focus on God necessitates trusting God, and to trust God means that you believe *the good shepherd will guide you every step of the way.*[47] Therefore, despite how the path might currently appear to you, trust that you are on the right path, and that God can work all things on the path into a pattern for your good.[48] This is the faith-walk God calls you to undertake upon the great adventure of your life.

MARCH 26

"No weapon formed against you shall prosper."

— Isaiah 54:17

Be still and receive the peace of God. The best way to receive God's peace is to become physically still. When your body is still, your mind will eventually follow. Once your mind is still, the radiance of God's love is released within you. When you trust God in any given area of your life, you allow the infinite correlating power of God's Universe to work in your favor. In contrast, when you try to single-handedly force solutions on problems, you only create more problems. God is able to demolish any stronghold formed against you. Rejoice, have faith, and entrust your life into His loving hands.

MARCH 27

*"You are always with me; You hold me by my
right hand. You guide me with your counsel,
and afterward you will take me to glory."*
— Romans 8:9

In the early morning hours, allow God to renew your mind, body and spirit. The setbacks, failures and disappointments of yesterday are forgiven, and a bright future awaits you. Begin each day anew, seeking the Kingdom of God which is alive within you. God is desirous to *hold you by your right hand*, and lead you along paths of righteousness.

MARCH 28

*"Cast your burden on the Lord, and He will sustain you.
He shall never permit the righteous to be moved."*

— Psalm 55:22

Regardless of what challenges you might be facing, *God is able to sustain you and carry you through them.* When you feel weighed down by a burden that is too heavy for you alone, develop the ability to surrender. In these moments of release, you do not surrender to the problem, challenge, or circumstance. Instead, you surrender to God, and gratefully entrust His mighty hand to lift your mind, body, and soul. When you surrender to God, you acknowledge that He has the reigns, that He is absolutely sovereign, and that the outcomes are ultimately in His hands. As you surrender, you also trust that *God will provide all your needs.* Everything you are experiencing now is for your ultimate good. Trust in God's unfailing love, and let Him carry your heavy load.

MARCH 29

"Have faith and knowledge resting on the hope of eternal life, which God, who does not lie, promised before the beginning of time."

— Titus 1:2

God's radiant knowledge and restorative power is available to you. Many times, you fall victim to the illusion of self-sufficiency, self-entitlement and ego-centric independence. Your ability to utilize your intellect and physical assets will only take you so far in life. However, real abundance, prosperity, power, strength, peace, knowledge, and wisdom are available exclusively with God. When you become still in God's presence, He will transform every fiber of your being. He will renew your mind, cleanse your heart, and invigorate your body. *He will lift you up upon the wings of an eagle, you will run and not grow weary.*[49] Brilliant vistas will open within your heart, and the comfort of God's presence will envelop you like a cool breeze. Then you will proclaim, *"Surely goodness will follow me all the days of my life."*[50]

MARCH 30

*"I have come that they may have life,
and have it more abundantly."*

— John 10:10

The closer you grow to God, the more you allow His infinite source of abundance to supply all your needs. This is why in the Bible, Jesus Christ taught his disciples to pray that God would, *"Give us our daily bread."*[51] When you are living from your spiritual center, God will supply all your necessary *worldly bread* in the form of the material objects required for the fulfillment of your life purpose. However, and even more importantly, God will also supply you with *Spiritual Bread*, for you cannot live on *worldly bread* alone.[52] This is one of the great secrets God desperately wants you to know. Instead of striving for worldly possessions in an effort to become happy and fulfilled, seek God and His Kingdom, and all the other details of your life will be accounted for.[53]

MARCH 31

"Be joyful in hope, patient in affliction, faithful in prayer."

— Romans 12:12

Develop the discipline to view challenging circumstances as an opportunity to draw closer to God. You have a tendency to resist things you do not want. When things do not go according to your plan, you lash out and ready yourself for battle. Instead of attempting to take charge of problems that arise in your awareness, focus your eyes on God and become receptive to His unfailing love. What you perceive as a problem is actually neutral; it is your thoughts about the situation that are the cause of suffering. Therefore, learn to direct your thoughts to God, and cast all your fear and anxiety on Him. God is watching over you continually, and He is always a safe resting place for you mind, body, and soul.

APRIL

"Jesus answered and said to him, 'If anyone loves me, he will keep my word; and my Father will love him, and We will come to him and make Our abode with him.'"

— John 14:23

APRIL 1

"Taste and see that the LORD is good;
blessed is the one who takes refuge in Him."
— Psalm 34:8

You have a divinely appointed ability to witness the quality of your thinking. In any given moment of your life, you can become this witness, and simply observe the habits of your mind. This ability to witness and observe yourself thinking creates a small space, or gap, between your witnessing self, and your actual thoughts. In this space lies the Peace of God. Learn to cultivate this space in the early morning hours as you sit silent and still in the presence of God. Over time and with practice, you will notice the gap between thoughts and the presence of God expanding within your mind. God's gentle caress will wash over you like a cooling mist, covering you with His peace. As you journey through the adventures of your day, this shield-like covering will protect your mind, allowing you to spontaneously make the right decisions. *Blessed and happy is the one who takes refuge in the peace of God.*

APRIL 2

"Be of sober spirit, and be on the alert. Your adversary, the devil, prowls around like a roaring lion, seeking someone to devour."

— 1 Peter 5:8

When you trust God, you take refuge in His protective embrace. Trusting God is more than a matter of your words; it is a matter of your willpower. As you journey through the adventures of this day, you will encounter things that make you anxious, including your own thinking. If you are not alert, you will unconsciously and unskillfully react to these circumstances, which will only lead to greater anxiousness and pain. Therefore, as Jesus Christ taught in the Bible, *"Be on alert at all times."*[54] You must use your willpower to remain on alert, and "catch" the negative worry-thoughts before they take hold of you. When you are careful, alert, and witnessing, you can take refuge in God, and the sacred space between your thoughts. In this space, God will elevate your perspective, and gently guide the quality of your thoughts. *In the shadow of God's wings, take refuge until the calamities have passed by.*[55]

APRIL 3

"This is the message we have heard: God is light, in Him there is no darkness at all. If we walk in the light, as He is in the light, we will have fellowship with one another."

— John 1:5-8

God is with you, all around you, and continually at work in your life. *The presence of God is overall, through all and in all.*[56] When you become aware of God's presence, you immediately begin to receive His healing and restorative power. As you remain aware, His love will continue to shine within you and through you. The Light of God in you has immense creative potential, and through this Light, you can do great things. *You can do all things through Christ, who strengthens you.*[57]

APRIL 4

"For everyone who asks and keeps on asking will receive; and he who seeks and keeps on seeking will find; and to him who knocks and keeps on knocking, the door shall be opened."

— Luke 11:10

When you pray in Jesus Christ's name with endurance, faith, and perseverance, you can accomplish great things. However, before you can receive, you must make contact with God's presence within you. This is why Jesus Christ taught his disciples to, *"Seek first the Kingdom of God, and everything else will be added to you."*[58] Instead of focusing on what you desire, bring your attention to the *One who is able to provide abundantly more than you can ask or imagine.*[59] As you begin to ponder the infinite and limitless creative ability of God, you will begin to discern which desires of your heart are in alignment with God's purpose in your life. When the desires of your heart match the purpose of your life, everything you ask for will be given to you.

APRIL 5

"Now to Him who is able to do exceedingly abundantly above all that we ask or think, according to the power that works in us.
— Ephesians 3:20

There is nothing you can do to make God love you more. Understanding this truthful awareness of God's unending and unconditional love is the first step in the attainment of your heart's desires. Any worldly limitation you currently have is a direct result of your limited thinking, not a limitation of God's love for you or His infinite ability to provide. God is both the creation and source of provision for what you ask. Your task is to dare to ask great things of God. As you ask and prepare to receive, your expectation will determine what God allows into your life. Your expectation will always perfectly match what you are able to receive. Therefore, allow God's love for you to inspire your expectation. *Whatsoever you ask for, believe you are worthy of receiving it, and it shall be yours.*[60]

APRIL 6

"The name of the LORD is a strong tower;
the righteous run to it and are safe."

— Proverbs 18:10

You can learn to live from a place of strength in God. Since God is both with you and for you, *His strong tower* is always one breath away from welcoming you home. When you view life from the perspective of God's fortress, and remain centered in His presence, you will handle problems with a light touch. When you realize you have wandered out from the security of *His tower*, return to Him by whispering, *"Help me, God."* When you call upon the name of God, you are immediately reconnected with Him, and will begin to feel the safety of His holy presence. The ability to notice you have wandered from God, and then reconnect to His presence, is a skill that takes persistent use of willpower to strengthen. However, the effort is worth the joyful gain you will receive when the skill is acquired. *Return to the strong tower of the LORD, and remain safely there.*

APRIL 7

"Trust in Him at all times. Pour out your hearts to Him, for God is your refuge."

— Psalm 62:8

Giving and receiving are two sides of the same coin. As you walk carefully along the adventurous paths of life, extend your hand to the Lord, and allow Him to *rejoice over you with gladness.*[61] Pray continually through the Holy Spirit within you to receive God's glorious love in full measure. In any given moment of your life, you can choose to *pour out your heart to God.* To surrender to God at all times is a testimony of spiritual strength. To trust God at all times is a testimony of spiritual faith. To love God at all times is a testimony of spiritual maturity.

APRIL 8

"The LORD your God is in your midst, the Mighty One will save you. He will rejoice over you with gladness, He will quiet you with His love, He will rejoice over you with singing."

— Zephaniah 3:17

God is conditioning you to remain close to Him. Every moment of your life is an opportunity for you to witness the presence of God. When times are good, and everything seems to be going your way, it is easy to focus exclusively on your worldly success. Similarly, when you face challenging times, it is easy to focus exclusively on the trials and tribulations you are struggling with. God is desirous of your attention in all the moments and seasons of your life. God wants you to focus on Him during circumstances you perceive as both good and bad. Ultimately, you will mature to the realization that nothing is good or bad, positive or negative; but your thinking makes it so. When you grasp the reality that everything you attract into your life is for your benefit, then you will understand the Scripture, *"For my God supplies all I need, according to His riches in the glory of Christ Jesus."*[62]

APRIL 9

"Love the LORD your God, listen to His voice, and hold fast to Him. For the LORD is your life, and will give you many years in the land He swore to your fathers."
— Deuteronomy 30:20

God wants to have a very real relationship with you. In any relationship, there are certain qualities that lend themselves to intimacy, love, and closeness. Among these qualities is the sacrifice of time. Your use of time is an indicator of where you are directing your attention. How much time do you spend with God each day? Is the amount of time you spend with God enough to enhance the quality of the relationship He wants to have with you? These are potentially life-changing questions to contemplate. Spend time each day pouring your heart out to God. Learn to hold tightly to His hand and seek out His refuge during the idle moments of your day. As you draw close to God, you will notice God drawing close to you. As you remain in constant dialogue with God, you will become aware of His voice and gentle direction in your life. *Hold fast to God, for He is your life.*

APRIL 10

"I have set the LORD always before me. Because He is at my right hand, I will not be shaken."

— Psalm 16:8

If you want to build anything meaningful in your life, whether it be a business or a marriage, you must first create a strong foundation. This is why Jesus Christ taught his disciples the significance of *building your home on a rock.*[63] Imagine the power of your life if everything you did was both for the glory of God, and was created on the rock of His Word. When you walk steadily with God and glorify Him in everything you say and do, a power will radiate through you that will light the world. You are a child of God, and were created for mighty things. Let your life be a testimony to your love for God, and God will testify His love for you.

APRIL 11

"These things I have spoken to you, that in me you may have peace. In the world you will have tribulation; but be of good cheer, I have overcome the world."
— John 16:33

Your mind has a tendency to jump to the future, or regress to the past. However, God is only available to you in the present moment you are now experiencing. When you find yourself in any place other than this very moment, take a breath and relax into the presence of God. Your breath can become an anchor to the present-moment, because when you bring your awareness to your breath, you are breathing now. It is simply not possible for you to breath tomorrow, or yesterday. You can only breath now. God designed you to anchor your awareness to the present moment through the breath. To witness the presence of God, take the following steps as often as necessary:

1. Take a deep breath in.

2. Take a slow breath out.

3. Witness the peace of God.

APRIL 12

"Humble yourselves, therefore, under God's mighty hand, that He may lift you up in due time. Cast all your anxiety on Him because He cares for you."

— 1 Peter 5:6-7

At certain times, the conditions of your life cause you to feel defeated, weighted down, and powerless to change things. In these moments, the habit of your mind is to focus on the uncomfortable position you are in. You must remember that what you focus your attention on will only increase in your life. Therefore, instead of focusing on the unpleasant conditions of your life, focus on God. Your discomfort can be a wake-up call and can jump-start your faith in God. The more you affirm your trust in the Lord, the more God can bless you with His unfailing love. Have humbleness, perseverance, stamina, and endurance in trusting God, and He will lift up your life *according to His glory and mighty riches.*[64]

APRIL 13

*"You will show me the path of life; in Your
presence is fullness of joy; at Your right
hand are pleasures forevermore."*
— Psalm 16:11

You must learn to discipline what you are focusing your attention upon. In the world around you, there are both magnificent vistas of beauty, as well as dark wastelands. When you focus on what is *true, righteous, lovely, noble, and lovely*, you will find hope, encouragement, and strength.[65] God created you with the ability to focus your attention in such a manner that you would enjoy beauty, wellness, goodness, and true prosperity. Therefore, an important prayer is the humble request that *your spiritual eyes would be opened to the presence of God.*[66] Also, remember the world will never fully satisfy your longing. God alone is the fulfillment of your deepest need for completion and wholeness. God is perfect in every way. God is holy in every way. God is sufficient in every way. Focus your eyes and attention on God, and *His presence overflow your cup of abundance.*[67]

APRIL 14

*"He who dwells in the shelter of the Most High
will rest in the shadow of the Almighty."*

— Psalm 91:1

The God whom you love, and who loves you, is a mighty God. *He is a mighty warrior who saves.*[68] Whenever you are weary or exhausted, be still and whisper this prayer: *"Help me, God."* God's eternal promise is that He will fight for you, however you must first become still, and allow God the opportunity to enter the battle. When you are struggling to keep your head above water, you tend to feel that your struggling is what is keeping you alive. The more you struggle, the more exhausted you become, until you finally surrender and ask God for help. Discipline yourself to win the battles of life without struggle. Make a daily devotion of welcoming the presence of God into your life. Let God be your first priority, and not your last resort.

APRIL 15

*"But thou art Holy, You that inhabit
the praises of Your people."*

— Psalm 22:3

You cannot possibly praise or thank the Lord your God enough. However, your tendency is to praise God based on circumstances you judge as favorable and praiseworthy. Praising God as a spontaneous response to His blessings is only a start. In addition, when goodness is abundant in your life, it is easy to mistake your individual effort and hard work for the grace and mercy of God. You must realize that praise is a matter of the heart, and a matter of your willpower. Learn to praise and affirm your trust in God at all times and under all circumstances. In idle moments of your life, direct your attention to the Giver of all gifts, and offer thanksgiving for the subtle blessings in your life. Take a deep breath in, and a slow breath out. Slowly open and close your eyes. Open and close the palms of your hands. Listen to the sound of your voice. Praise God.

APRIL 16

"But for me it is good to be near God; I have made the
LORD God my refuge, that I may tell of all Your works."
— Psalm 73:28

Your ability to witness the presence of God has more to do with feeling than thinking. God designed you to inhabit the Holy Spirit as a felt experience. God is desirous of the feelings in your heart. In the same manner that you *feel love* for a spouse, child, parent, friend, or sibling, you can feel love for God. Every quality that enhances the intimacy of a human relationship can equally enhance your intimacy with God. You must spend an equal amount of time *feeling love for God, as you do feeling God's love for you.* To conjure up the feeling and emotion of love for God, imagine yourself embracing His Son, Jesus Christ. *It is good to be near the Lord your God.*

APRIL 17

*"Therefore do not worry about tomorrow,
for tomorrow will worry about itself. Each
day has enough trouble of its own."*

— Matthew 6:34

If you wait to praise God until it occurs to you, worldly distractions will inhibit the intimacy He is desirous of. God *is infinite and is the same yesterday, today, and forevermore.*[69] However, you are limited to this moment. You exist in the now; you always have, and you always will. Therefore, the time for you to commune with God *will always be now.* God will equip you to be victorious in every situation; you simply have to become aware of His presence. When you live dependently on God, trusting Him in every moment of your life, He will strengthen you. He will hold your hand, and prepare the way for you. *Tomorrow is busy worrying about itself.* Trust God one day at a time.

APRIL 18

"In everything you do, put God first, and He will direct you and crown your efforts with success."

— Psalm 3:6

God created a Universe that resides in perfect alignment with the *Law of Order*. Therefore, you must discipline yourself to act in accordance with God's Law, and trust Him in every area of your life. The first step in trusting God and aligning with the Law of Order is to *put God first in everything you say and do*.[70] God's Law of Order simply means to prioritize *what is important over what is not important*. God is more important than anything or anyone in the world.

APRIL 19

"Remain in me and I will remain in you. No branch can bear fruit by itself; it must remain in the vine."

— John 15:4

Spending time silent, still, and alone with God can be challenging for you. This is largely due to worldly conditioning which places value on activity, busyness, and task-prioritized accomplishments. However, *storing up your treasures in Heaven has more to do with stillness than action.* God is desirous of your time and attention. Nothing you accomplish in the world could possibly make God love you more. Therefore, live close to God, and learn to bask in the warmth of His embrace. Stay with God a little bit longer today and notice the Peace of His presence.

APRIL 20

---

*"Blessed are they which do hunger and thirst
for righteousness: for they shall be filled."*

— Matthew 5:6

The words "hunger" and "thirst" provide insight into your desire for spiritual fulfillment. Nothing in the world, and nothing of the world, will ever fully satisfy you. Deep inside your heart, this truth patiently resides, silently awaiting your awakening to the salvation only God can provide. When you develop a deep hunger and thirst for communion with God, your life will be blessed in a profoundly positive way. God will fill the emptiness within you, and His lasting happiness will comfort you all the days of your life. *Delight yourself in the LORD, and He will give you the desires of your heart.*[71]

APRIL 21

"The LORD is my portion, therefore I have hope in Him."
— Lamentations 3:24

In order to attract anything into your life, you must focus your mind upon exactly what it is you desire. Your mind has immense magnetic pulling-power, and over time, everything that is within the magnetic force field of your mind will become your reality. You must remember that your power to attract and magnetize does not have an ability to discern the quality of what it attracts. The pulling-power of your mind will simply draw towards itself anything it focuses upon. Therefore, discipline yourself to continually evaluate the conditions of your life in order to assess what you have been focusing on and thinking about. Focus your mind upon God, and He will direct the conditions of your life. When God becomes the sole center-point of your thinking, *goodness will surely accompany you all the days of your life.*[72]

APRIL 22

"But the fruit of the Spirit is love, joy, peace, patience, kindness, goodness, faithfulness, gentleness and self-control."

— Galatians 5:22-23

You must develop the ability to connect with your spiritual self. At the center of your being resides the presence of God. When your thinking arises from within His presence, the qualities of peace, love, kindness, and self-control will be yours.

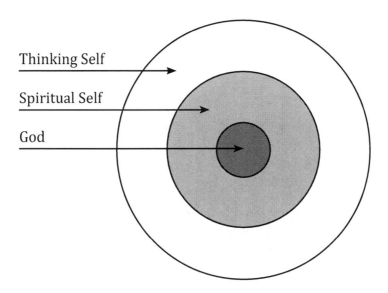

Thinking Self

Spiritual Self

God

APRIL 23

"Come to me, all you who are weary and burdened, and I will give you rest. Take my yoke upon you and learn from me, for I am gentle and humble in heart, and you will find rest for your souls."

— Matthew 11:28-29

Your frame of mind will influence everything that you behold. The same set of facts, when viewed from either a positive or negative state of mind, will be perceived in such a manner as to either bring pleasure or pain. When you view the world through the presence of God, your perspective will change in a dramatic way. Problems will no longer discourage you, and instead will be reminders to seek the peace, comfort, and security of God. Joyous circumstances will be magnified as you praise God for the blessings He bestowed upon you. Come to God when you are *weary and burdened*. Come to God when you are *happy and delighted*. Allow God to *be the anchor of your soul through all the days of your life*.[73]

APRIL 24

*"Love the LORD your God, and keep His requirements,
His decrees, His Laws, and His commands at all times."*

— Deuteronomy 11:1

Horses in Arabia go through a rigorous selection process. To live in the hot, dry, and austere desert climate, a rider depends on the unfailing obedience of their horse. Arabian horses are tested in such a way as to select only the very best. For one particular test, the horses are worked hard for three days with no food and very little water. At the end of the three days, they are placed next to a corral gate with troughs of clear water and hay. When the gate opens, the horses gallop towards the troughs. Just as the first horses reach the trough, a whistle is sounded for the horses to return. The horses that take a quick drink before returning to their masters are eliminated from further testing. The horses that are chosen are those that without hesitation obey their master's command and return.

APRIL 25

"Do not be conformed to this world, but be transformed by the renewal of your mind."

— Romans 12:2

God is with you. He is hovering over you, aware of your every thought. You tend to think thoughts are fleeting and unimportant. However, nothing could be further from the Truth. As your thinking goes, so goes your entire world. Develop the discipline of internally repeating God's Word, planting within your subconscious the seeds of peacefulness, happiness, abundance, and joy. *Delight yourself in the LORD, and He will give you the desires of your heart.*[74]

APRIL 26

"Let us fix our eyes on Jesus, the author and perfecter of our faith, who for the joy set before him endured the cross, scorning its shame, and sat down at the right hand of the throne of God."

— Hebrews 12:2

Fix your eyes on Jesus Christ, for He is the one who remains the same. You have a tendency to focus your attention upon the matters of the world. Like an ocean during a storm, the matters of the world are constantly tossing about, changing direction, and in a perpetually unsteady state. Welcome God into your life, and He will come to you and you will realize that He is the Ocean of Life, and that you are a tiny wave, and that you are one with the Ocean. You must continue to practice the skill of turning your attention inward, and concentrate upon the part of you that is always still, and always the same. Although a *still small voice*, God's presence is within you at all times, and under all circumstances. There is nothing you can do, and no place you can go, that would distance you from God's love.

APRIL 27

"Let us hold fast the confession of our hope without wavering, for He who promised is faithful."
— Hebrews 10:23

Where your eyes go, your whole body will follow. As true as this statement is in athletics, its implications for your entire life are even greater. You will gravitate towards whatever it is you are looking at, thinking about, talking about, and focusing upon. Of the infinite number of objects to focus upon, only One will provide you with everything you need, both on Heaven and Earth. Even a quick glance in the direction of God can help to redirect the course of your day into safer waters. Retain a peripheral awareness of the world, and the events taking place around you. However, your primary focus should be upon God. When the majority of your thinking, speaking, and feeling is in the presence of God, your life will reach a tipping point of divine proportion.

APRIL 28

*"Now faith is confidence in what we hope
for and assurance about what we do not see."*

— Hebrews 11:1

God wants to teach you about the essence of eternal value. The world wants to teach you about momentary and fleeting objects of desire. True wisdom lies in your ability to discern the difference. As you identify more fully with God, you will begin to understand what holds eternal and lasting value, and what is simply a thought wave passing though the ocean of your awareness. As thoughts come and thoughts go, observe them without attachment. Learn to appreciate the rhythm of life, which is evident in nature all around you.

Seasons come and go.

Thoughts come and go.

Emotions come and go.

People come and go.

God is forever.

APRIL 29

"The LORD will stay with you as long as you stay with Him. Whenever you look for Him, you will find Him."

— 2 Chronicles 15:2

Jesus Christ taught a key lesson that can benefit your life each day: *Seek and you will find.* This promise means that whenever and wherever you look for God, you will find Him. God's promise is to be with you always. Even in difficult moments, when you feel all alone, God is within you, and protectively standing by your side. In order to really feel into the presence of God, you must engage your willpower and wield the sword of faith to cut through distractions, deception, and discouragement. The sword of faith is sharpest when you speak the *Word of God.* Memorize God's mighty Word, and repeat His promises throughout the day. God's Word shall be your armor, and His truth will set you free.

APRIL 30

"Today is the day the LORD has made,
we will rejoice and be glad in it."
— Psalm 118:24

You were made to face challenging circumstances only once, and that is when they are actually occurring. God designed you this way, because He wanted to be with you during both the glorious and difficult moments of your life. Although God is omnipotent, and has reach beyond your understanding of time, *you are always only here, and only now*. God cannot reach you yesterday, and He cannot reach you tomorrow. He can only be with you today, and in this very moment. When you spend time worrying about what could happen in the future, or rehash events that happened in the past, you increase the felt experience of suffering in your life. However, when you spend time *here and now*, in communion with God, you experience peacefulness, rest, and rejuvenation. God will strengthen and prepare you to handle one day at a time. *For today is the day the Lord has made, let us rejoice and be glad in it.*

MAY

---

*"Do you not know that you are a temple of God
and that the Spirit of God dwells in you?"*

— 1 Corinthians 3:16

MAY 1

"Seek the LORD and His strength;
seek His face evermore."

— Psalm 105:4

You tend to feel at the mercy of your life circumstances, and the conditions of your life often determine your ability to witness the presence of God. However, you can learn to behold the presence of God and His love during the ebb and flow of your life. God's love for you is so powerful it can pierce through both difficult and celebratory times, and is not dependent upon how you feel. God's presence in your life can be the center-point from which emotions and feelings arise. God is the rock you can safely stand upon, despite the current of life's great ocean. When you feel distant from God—it's not God who moved. Return to the peace within you. God is always just a breath away from welcoming you home.

MAY 2

"The mind controlled by the Spirit is life and peace."
— Romans 8:6

As a child of God, you are blessed with divine manifesting potential. At birth, God infused you with the skills and abilities of an architect. The building blocks of your life are your thoughts, words, and actions. Every day you have an opportunity to use the power of your thinking to create beauty, abundance, and health. Every day you have a renewed chance to speak into God's Universe affirmations of prosperity, love, and kindness. Every day you have an ability to perform acts of devotion, service, and justice. *Lift up your eyes to the LORD, and constantly proclaim His good name.*[75]

MAY 3

"In this world you will have trouble. But
take heart, Christ has overcome the world!"

— John 16:33

During challenging and difficult times, do not mistake the problem for your *thinking about the problem*. When experiences arise in your awareness, the habit of your mind is to label them as either good or bad. As you continue to mature in your relationship with God, you will learn to see everything through the perspective of Jesus Christ. Once you realize everything that you experience is ultimately for your good, you can begin to commune with God, and ask His spirit to guide your thinking. Your thinking affects your life like a perfect karmic accounting system. Every thought you have, and every word you speak adds to a permanent mosaic, and your actions ripple through the fertile manifesting soil of God's Universe. In time, you will experience the harvest of every karmic seed you plant, and in this sense, you can experience the joy of Heaven on Earth. Therefore, draw close to God, and ask Him to show you the opportunity and blessing in every moment of your life.

MAY 4

"For man looks on the outward appearance,
but the LORD looks on the heart."

— 1 Samuel 16:7

God is within you, and all around you. In order to connect with the presence of God, you must move from *thinking to feeling*. God's presence is felt in your heart rather than comprehended in your mind. When you learn to identify with your feelings, you will have moved a step closer to a heart like Jesus Christ. This is because feelings and emotions contain magnetic power that attract like thoughts, words, and actions. When you feel good, you tend to draw into your life conditions that match your feeling. When you feel good, your thoughts and words reflect love, kindness, positivity, and optimism. When you feel good, the light of God shines through you into the world.

MAY 5

*"Trust in the LORD forever, for
the LORD is the Rock eternal."*

— 1 Isaiah 26:4

God is asking you to trust Him during every moment of your life. Trusting God for a little while is easy, especially when things seem to be going well for you. However, God is asking for eternal trust that transcends the conditions of your life. God wants to be your strong rock, capable of sustaining and supporting you at all times. Although your trust will fluctuate, God remains the same, and does not judge or condemn your tendency to wobble. You must remember that the invisible universe of thought, feeling, emotion, and attitude will become visible as a consequence of your mind's ability to attract the prevailing and habitual thinking, speaking, and feeling patterns you entertain. The principle involved is that *what is seen was not made out of things that are visible.*[76] Therefore, instead of thinking and speaking of the difficult conditions of your life, think and speak of God and His perfect love for you.

MAY 6

"Come to me, all you who labor and are heavy laden, and I will give you rest."

— Matthew 11:28

Imagine for a moment the qualities of a rock. A rock is strong, and capable of holding weight placed upon it. A rock can easily weather a storm. The conditions of the earth are subject to change, yet a rock remains the same. *A wise man builds his house upon a rock, so that when a storm comes and waters rise, his home will remain safe.*[77] These are but a few of the reasons Jesus Christ used the metaphor of a rock when describing the eternal qualities of God. Are you treating God as your precious rock? God can easily bear any burden you might be holding. God invites you to lean upon Him, and rest in the safety of His protective strength. When you are feeling *heavy laden with worries*, come to the Lord, and trust Him with your heart and mind.

MAY 7

*"Lean on, and be confident in the LORD
with all your heart and mind."*

— Proverbs 3:5

Self-pity is a grave danger in your life. When you are experiencing unrest, struggle, and unease, the trap of negativity is like a downward spiral, pulling you into increasingly troubled waters. Because the mind and body are so closely connected, develop the habit of maintaining good physical posture and proper breathing techniques. Your mind will surely follow the upright alignment of your body. To protect the mind, also learn to continually *fix your eyes upon the LORD.*[78] The closer you live to the light of God, the more distance you create between the darkness. God's presence will equip you for the great adventure that this day holds. His light will glorify the path set before you, and His mighty hand will lift your heart.

MAY 8

"For God so loved the world, that He gave His only Son, that whoever believes in him should not perish but have eternal life."

— John 3:16

In order to accomplish any goal in your life, first you must develop the belief you are capable of achieving the goal. The only difference between the person who achieves a particular goal, and the person who fails, is the person who achieved first believed they could. Now, considering the power of personal belief, imagine the potential that awaits when you realize the presence of God within you is far more capable than you without God. For this reason, the Bible teaches: *Through Christ, you can do all things.*[79] Any endeavor or challenge, regardless how imposing or grand in nature, is never yours alone. Everything can be accomplished with the Spirit of God within you. Allow your internal compass to guide you to a life of happiness and success by aligning with this Truth: *Be confident in the Lord, and do not rely on your own insight, capability, or understanding.*[80]

MAY 9

*"The LORD your God is in your midst. He
will rejoice over you with gladness."*
— Zephaniah 3:17

God is the source of every good gift in your life. *The greatest gift
God has in store for you is the renewing of your mind.*[81] When you
become still and silent in the majestic power of God's presence, you
are able to receive His healing, restoration, and heavenly perspective. In addition to your bountiful receiving, God rejoices in these
moments with you. Just like any worldly loved one, God is grateful for the time you spend with Him. God longs for quiet moments
with you. He wants to share a sunrise with you, and hopes to meet
with you again before retiring at night. Love and comfort go hand
in hand: When you love the Lord your God, you will experience the
comfort of a warm embrace and the restoration of your soul.

MAY 10

"May your unfailing love be my comfort,
according to your promise."

— Psalm 119:76

Young children instinctively turn to their parents during moments of fatigue, danger, and need. Somewhere during the course of your life, this self-evident truth was forgotten. Your tendency now is to struggle against the weight of your troubles. You forget that in any given moment, God is willing and able to carry the burden weighing you down. However, before God will step in, first you must recognize your neediness, and surrender to His embrace. The moment you confess, *"God, help me"* you will be redeemed. The strength of God will be upon you, and His everlasting love will warmly lift your heart and mind.

MAY 11

"The LORD gives strength to the weary and increases the power of the weak. Even youths grow tired and weary, and young men stumble and fall; but those who hope in the Lord will renew their strength. They will soar on wings like eagles; they will run and not grow weary, they will walk and not be faint."

— Isaiah 40:29-31

When your mind becomes like a still body of water, you are able to see the world through the eyes of Jesus Christ. To still your mind, you must first still your body. Each morning, develop the discipline to sit quietly in the presence of God. As your body begins to relax, the chatter of your mind will relax as well. Soon, your mind will take on the qualities of a polished mirror, capable of reflecting the presence of God within you. As God's face shines both in you and upon you, you will discover the peace of His promise.

MAY 12

"Now to Him who is able to do immeasurably more than all we ask or imagine, according to His power that is at work within us."

— Ephesians 3:20

Do not let anything disturb the peace within you. The more challenging the set of circumstances you face, the more strength God will provide. This understanding can form the basis for an unshakeable confidence and courage. God knows what challenges you will face each day, and He is eager to equip you for the great adventures of your life. Your part is to look to God for strength, and not rely on your limited understanding or capacity. Trust that God will never allow you to face an obstacle that you cannot overcome. Every circumstance and situation in your life will perfectly match your ability to be victorious over it.

MAY 13

*"In the morning, Oh LORD, you hear my voice;
in the morning I lay my requests before you
and wait in expectation."*

— Psalm 5:3

God is able to do more than you could ever ask or imagine. Your challenge is to experience life through the perspective of Christ, rather than your own limited understanding. God is continually at work in your life. He is both hovering over you, and is on the path slightly ahead of you, preparing the way. You are taking in life one experience at a time. However, God has your big picture in mind, and is continually bringing you one step closer to your prayers and requests. The great secret to receiving your heartfelt prayers is to continually thank God for their receipt, trusting that in His perfect time, *you will receive immeasurably more than you can ask for or imagine.*[82]

MAY 14

"So the LORD must wait for you to come to Him so He can show you His love and compassion. Blessed are those who wait for His help. He will be gracious if you ask for help. He will surely respond to the sound of your cries."

— Isaiah 30:18-19

The longer you wait to ask God for help, the more effort it will take on your part. Therefore, approach God gently each morning, and lay out your hopes, dreams, goals, prayers, and expectations for the day. You will be tempted to rush through this process, and jump into the day by the strength of your own means. However, you must remember that God did not create you to handle anything alone. God wants to be your partner, your friend, and your companion. He wants to work collaboratively with you to provide everything you need.

MAY 15

"Be strong and courageous. Do not be afraid or terrified because of them, for the LORD your God goes with you; He will never leave you nor forsake you."

— Deuteronomy 31:6

"Courage" comes from the French word meaning, *"Open hearted."* When God calls for you to be courageous, He is asking you to open your heart to His mighty presence. God is well aware of your circumstances, challenges, hopes, and dreams. God takes pleasure in providing for you. Notice how happy it makes you feel when a loved one asks you for help. For this reason, eagerly come to God with the requests of your heart, asking for His help in all matters. God takes pleasure in you always, but He is especially pleased when you take hope in Him, and seek *His steadfast love.*

MAY 16

"I am the door. If anyone enters by me, he will be saved, and will go in and out and find pasture. I have come that they may have life, and that they may have it more abundantly."

— John 10:7-10

God is in the space between your thoughts. When you become still in His presence, the space between your thoughts will gradually expand. This expansion will lead to a greater awareness of God's presence within you. God will fill your mind and heart with a tranquil peacefulness unlike anything you have ever known. Rest in the warmth of God's unconditional love. Receive His glorious strength, and allow ever fiber of your being to bask in the light of His embrace. *God will fill you with joy and peace, so that you will bubble over with hope by the power of Christ.*[83]

MAY 17

"Let us hold unswervingly to the hope we profess, for He who promised is faithful."
— Hebrews 10:23

God sent His Son, Jesus Christ, so that you would have life, and have it more abundantly. Christ's primary mission was to secure your eternal life. However, you do not need to wait until death to experience the joy of God's Kingdom. God wants you to have both eternal life in Heaven, and an abundantly joyful life today, and all the days in-between. This is why the Bible teaches you to: *"Rejoice and be glad, for today is the day the LORD has made."* As you draw close to God, and God draws close to you, the qualities of His Son will surely become part of you. Learn to be comfortable in the felt experience of happiness, joy, abundance, and prosperity. These feeling-states are your birthright, and God intends for you to experience them. Continually give praise and worship to God, and He will continually give you reason for thanksgiving.

MAY 18

*"Your Word is a lamp to my feet
and a light for my path."*
— Psalm 119:05

The Word of God is alive with power, potential, and strength. Bible verse repeated both out loud and in the silence of your mind has the ability to heal your heart, and restore your weary soul. The more often you repeat God's Word, the greater His Word will be in your life. With any new skill, repetition is the first law of learning. When you have repeated God's Word so often that His voice plays like background music in your mind, then you will have made progress. Grace will become your natural state of being, and you will increasingly grow in the likeness of Jesus Christ.

MAY 19

"The Word of God is living and powerful, and sharper than any two-edged sword, piercing even to the division of soul and spirit, and of joints and marrow, and is a discerner of the thoughts and intents of the heart."

— Hebrews 4:12

A *double-edged sword* means a weapon that can cut in both directions. This is why God cautions you to wield the sword of the Word carefully. Everything you say has manifesting and creative potential in your life. Just as a two-edged sword is indifferent to what lies before its edge, your spoken word can either heal or hurt. Each word you speak spills into the fertile soil of God's Universe, and will produce accordingly. In time, by the Law of God, you will reap either the benefit or ill effect of every continually repeated thought, word and action. Therefore, let your thoughts temper your tongue, so that your word may bring glory to God, and goodwill into every corner of your life.

MAY 20

"The LORD will be your everlasting light,
and your God will be your glory."

— Isaiah 60:19

God created your mind in such a way that when you focus upon something, whatever you focus upon increases in size, clarity and magnitude. When you focus upon a problem, the problem will have the effect of moving closer to you, and expanding over your life. Similarly, when you focus on God, His presence will expand over your life, and His love will move closer to you. In any given moment, you have the innate ability to choose what you are focusing upon. Focus on God, and God will focus on you.

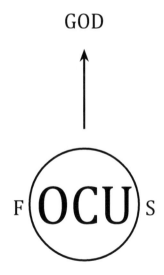

MAY 21

*"If you abide in my word, you are truly
my disciples, and you will know the truth,
and the truth will set you free."*

— John 8:31

You must continually refine your ability to hear the voice of God. In order to discern the voice of God from the competing voices within your mind, *simply move from thinking to feeling.* There is a way to listen with your heart, that with continued practice, you can fully develop. Your heart, feelings, and emotions are the place God desires to communicate with you. In any moment, simply ask yourself, *"Do I feel the presence of God?"* If the answer is yes, than trust the feelings and impulses within, and courageously follow your heart, which is God speaking to you. If the answer is no, than simply become still, and pray that God would reveal His presence to you. *God will never leave you or forsake you.*[84] When you feel distant from God, it was not God who moved. Return to His embrace, and the love of His everlasting presence.

MAY 22

"And He said 'My Presence will go with you, and I will give you rest.'"

— Exodus 33:14

God's presence is like a cloak of armor, protecting you from the sharp arrows of worldly troubles. Just like developing competency in a physical skill, you must take the necessary time to condition your mind to receive the Peace of God. When you make an effort to become still and focus on God, the habits of your mind will pull your attention away. When this happens, simply whisper, *"God, help me"* and return your awareness to your breath and your posture. Your breath and body can help anchor your awareness to the present moment, which is where God longs to meet you. With practice you will develop the ability to spend longer and longer periods of time fully concentrated upon God. This is what Jesus Christ meant when he said, *"The truth will set you free."* You will become free from all self-doubt and the illusion of separateness from God. You will rejoice in the tender embrace of His love, and will give thanksgiving for His protective presence.

MAY 23

"I will wait for the LORD, my soul waits, and in His Word I put my hope. My soul waits for the LORD more than watchmen wait for the morning."
— Psalm 130:5-6

A watchman stood guard atop a castle wall. With serene patience, he stood protectively through the long and weary night.

Still several hours before the hope of the rising sun, a young kingsmen approached the faithful guard and asked,

"How do you wait through the long hours of the dark night?"

The wise watchman replied,

"Although the night sometimes seems terribly long, I have learned it always ends with the dawn of morning. No matter how dark, the hope of the glorious rising sun lifts my spirit."

MAY 24

*"Now may the LORD of peace Himself give
you peace at all times and in every way.
May the peace of God be with you."*

— 2 Thessalonians 3:16

In this very moment, the Spirit of God is within you. As you take the next breath in, direct your attention to His everlasting presence. God is aware of your every thought, and longs to restore the quality of your mind. As your thinking goes, so goes your entire world. You are beginning to understand that thoughts are neither fleeting nor idle. On the contrary, thoughts are real, and contain within them creative potential, worthy of your respect and appreciation. Develop the discipline of internally repeating God's Word, planting within your subconscious the seeds of peacefulness, happiness, abundance, and joy. *Delight yourself in The Lord, and He will give you the pleasures of your heart.*[85]

MAY 25

"Peace I leave with you; my peace I give you."
— John 14:27

The presence of God results in the presence of peace. God wants to bestow His peace upon you *at all times and in every way.* You have a tendency to *search here and there for a resting place.* As long as you continue to search outside yourself for peace, your search for peace will never end. This is because there is a hole within you that can only be filled by God. In this sense, you are searching for something you already have. Many people do not recognize this, and therefore attempt to fill the void through possessions, relationships, and professional purists. In order to fill the gap, the first step is to realize you do not need to do anything. Rather, you simply need to receive the glorious gift of God's presence, which is already alive within you. This is why, shortly before his death, Jesus Christ promised his disciples peace. Christ intuitively knew his disciples would search for him, and the peace only God could provide. God will supply everything you need. Find peace in the presence of God within you, and gratefully receive the full measure of His blessing.

MAY 26

"In everything you do, put God first, and He will direct you and crown your efforts with success."

— Proverbs 3:6

God is conditioning you to develop the skill of steadiness. In the warrior culture, the greatest compliment to bestow upon another is the accolade of steadiness during danger. God wants you to remain aware of His presence at all times, and under all circumstances. Regardless of what is happening within you and all around you, God is desirous of your attention. Rather than allowing unexpected events to deter your course, remain steady and continually return your awareness to God. In this manner, God will rejoice in your joys, and strengthen you in troubled waters.

MAY 27

"The LORD is good to those who wait for Him, to the soul who seeks Him."

— Lamentations 3:25

The most important spiritual truth of your existence is that God is always with you. God is not limited by your understanding of space and time. God's presence is infinite, always the same, everlasting, and forevermore. Do not let the future cause you anxiety, for God is already there. You are always safely in the palm of His hand; *do not worry about what tomorrow will bring.*[86] Use the energy God gave you today to focus exclusively upon today. Although God is everywhere at all times, you are confined to the space and time dimensions of this very moment. Thankfully, this very moment is the place God is waiting for you. He is with you now.

MAY 28

"We know that in all things God works for the good of those who love Him, who have been called according to His purpose."

— Romans 8:28

God created you to accomplish great things. When you are in perfect alignment with God, inspiration, divine guidance, and creativity will become a natural state of being for you. When you use the God-given talents bestowed upon you, success and good fortune will effortlessly come to you. Just like stepping into a fast-moving river and allowing the current to carry you towards the ocean, you can step into energetic flow with God. When you allow God to flow through you, everything you do will be magnified for His glory.

MAY 29

"This is the message which we have heard from Him and declare to you, that God is light and in Him is no darkness at all."

— 1 John 1:5

If you want success, happiness, joy, prosperity, love, health, wholeness, and fitness, you must condition your mind to think exclusively of what you desire. Whatever you think about and talk about will become the reality of your life. Jesus Christ spoke of light, health, and life, and through the discriminative and disciplined use of his speech, he healed the sick and raised the dead. Learn to turn the creative and manifesting power of your thinking and speaking into a source of wellbeing. Praise God with everything you think, everything you say, and everything you do.

MAY 30

"As for God, His way is perfect; the Word of the LORD is proven. He is a shield to all who trust in Him."

— Psalm 18:30

As you identify more and more fully with God, His loving presence will become increasingly intertwined with yours. When you live close to God, you will feel the effects of the Spirit of Jesus Christ in you. Lightheartedness, kindness, positivity, and happiness will become the resting point of your days. People will gravitate towards you, and seek your comfort and encouragement. You will approach problems with a light touch, confident in every outcome. Let the presence of God shine through you, and His light will bring goodness into every corner of your life.

MAY 31

"I delight greatly in the LORD;
my soul rejoices in my God."

— Isaiah 61:10

Let nothing intimidate you or weigh you down. The greater the challenge before you, the greater the presence of God within you. You tend to think God empowers you equally for each day. However, this is not actually the case. Instead, God provides the exact amount of strength you need to overcome any set of circumstances. The degree to which God strengthens you is always in direct proportion to the help you require and ask Him for. Develop the confidence to look to God for everything you need, and then patiently wait for His works to bless your life.

JUNE

"We who have fled to Him for refuge can have great confidence as we hold to the hope that lies before us. This hope is a strong and trustworthy anchor for our souls. It leads us through the curtain into God's inner sanctuary."

— Hebrews 6:18-19

JUNE 1

"I am the LORD your God. I do not change."
— Malachi 3:6

There is a difference between seeking peace in God, and peace in the world. Seeking peace in the world is dependent upon external circumstances, events, people, and conditions. To seek peace in the world causes you frustration and anxiety. Any peace you happen across is fleeting and temporary, which ultimately leads to greater amounts of unrest and suffering. However, take heart, for your God overcame the world. Therefore, instead of seeking peace in the world, find comfort in the Prince of Peace, and take rest in His sovereign arms. Regardless of the torrent a storm may produce, the sky will return to blue, and the sun will shine again. Adverse conditions will come and go in the same manner. God is always the same, and His peace is always a safe place for your soul.

JUNE 2

"Pray in the Spirit on all occasions with all kinds of prayers and requests. With this in mind, be alert and keep on praying for all the saints."

— Ephesians 6:18

Spend the majority of your time in prayer. Unlike a worldly relationship in which communication is expressed through the action of touch and speech, communion with God can happen in the silence of your heart. Develop the discipline to steal away quiet moments with God during the course of your day. Revel in the felt experience of receiving God's embrace, which is surrounding you at all times and places. The more you direct your thoughts and feelings to God, the more alive and hopeful you will feel.

JUNE 3

*"He lifted me out of the slimy pit, out of
the mud and mire; He set my feet on a rock
and gave me a firm place to stand."*

— Psalm 40:2

God can be your swimming coach, or your lifeguard. The choice is up to you. In the great ocean of life's adventure, it is far better to learn how to swim. Take the time to receive God's grace, and understand the currents, rip tides, and means of navigating the ebb and flow of the sea. This is achieved through prayer and stillness in His presence. If you should decide to simply jump into the raging ocean, God will still be available to rescue you. You simply need to say, *"God, help me."* Therefore, whether you should decide to learn how to swim, or wait to be rescued, God is eager and willing to be at your side.

JUNE 4

"Be happy and rejoice and be glad-hearted. Be unceasing in prayer and thank God in all matters."

— 1 Thessalonians 5:16

There is a mighty power in your thoughts and words. The first step of the creative process always begins in your mind. A thought, repeated over time, will eventually produce a corresponding effect in your life. Similarly, creative energy resonates throughout God's Universe every time you speak. In other words, your thinking and speaking are like a blueprint that is projected onto the screen of life. Therefore, guard your thoughts and your tongue, disciplining yourself to honor the great teaching of Jesus Christ: *You shall reap what you sow.*[87] Ensure the seeds of your thoughts and words of your testimony are abundant in light, love, kindness, health, and positivity.

JUNE 5

"Therefore I will praise you, Oh LORD, among the nations; I will sing the praises of your name."
— 2 Samuel 22:50

When you praise God for the desires of your heart, the object of your desire immediately begins its wayward journey into your arms. In the creative process, this is known as the Law of Praise. Those who understand and apply this Law display a great understanding of faith in God. This is because the testimony of your faith in God is always measured before you receive, not afterwards. Therefore, you must learn to discern the difference between praising God for what you desire, and the lack of it. When you continually praise God for the desires of your heart, you will receive them. However, when you pray to God about the lack of what you desire, you will continue to receive that as well. Jesus Christ understood the Law of Praise, and used it to feed a crowd of five thousand people with five loaves of bread and two fish. *Jesus looked up to Heaven, gave thanks, and broke the bread. Then he gave them to his disciples, and his disciples gave them to the people.*[88]

JUNE 6

---

*"But you are a chosen people, a royal priesthood,
a holy nation, a people belonging to God, that you
may declare the praises of Him who called you out
of darkness into His wonderful light."*

— 1 Peter 2:9

There is a difference between desiring right circumstances, and your right response to whatever circumstances come your way. Jesus Christ taught his disciples they *should expect to experience problems in the world.*[89] Therefore, it is an unwise use of your energy to attempt to control circumstances out of your control. Instead of wasting time and resources trying to control people and events, dedicate yourself to improving the quality of your response to everything that is arising in your awareness. As circumstances enter into your life experience, pause for a moment before reacting. In this brief moment before stimulus and response lies the Peace of God. When you glorify God by becoming aware of His presence in the midst of circumstances, the Light of His love will elevate your perspective and provide you with comfort and wellbeing.

JUNE 7

*"Praise and glory and wisdom and thanks
and honor and power and strength be to
our God for ever and ever."*
— Revelation 7:12

The illusion of living a problem-free life is captivating. You have a tendency to spend time attempting to control and predict future events. Remember that God will perfectly equip you to handle whatever circumstances arise during the great adventures of your life. When you experience anxiety in your mind, bring your awareness to the cause of the uneasy feelings. You will discover that your mind is very powerful; it can create feelings of nervousness, unrest, and anxiety, even for events that have not yet happened and might never actually materialize. Your mind can create scenes that produce emotion, no different than watching a happy or sad movie. Therefore, learn to anchor your mind and soul to the present moment. *Let tomorrow worry about tomorrow.*

JUNE 8

"If anyone speaks, he should do it as one speaking the very words of God. If anyone serves, he should do it with the strength God provides, so that in all things God may be praised through Jesus Christ. To Him be the glory and the power for ever and ever."

— 1 Peter 4:11

Instead of seeking perfection, pour your energy into seeking God. Whatever you focus your attention on will increase in your life. Energy will flow from you onto the object of your attention. Therefore, let the chief desires of your heart be to love, glorify, and seek God. Learn to enjoy the presence of God at all times, and under every possible circumstance that arises in your awareness. Trust that everything you experience *is for your good.* When things seem to be going well, glorify and praise God for His goodness. When things seem to be going wrong, praise God anyway. Praise in the midst of trouble requires a supernatural faith, and this is the very faith God is desirous for you to achieve.

JUNE 9

"So then, just as you received Christ Jesus as Lord, continue to live in him, rooted and built up in him, strengthened in the faith as you were taught, and overflowing with thankfulness."

— 2 Colossians 2:6-7

When you walk along the path of life with God, you gain a higher perspective over your circumstances. You are able to see people and situations through the peacefulness that only His presence can provide. You will find the deeper and more intimate your relationship with God becomes, the higher the perspective you will gain over the world. God will lift your eyes and heart, providing you with understanding, compassion, and serenity. When you completely trust God with your life, an energetic gentleness, confidence, and peace will exude from you.

JUNE 10

"Do not be anxious about anything, but in everything, by prayer and petition, with thanksgiving, present your requests to God."
— Philippians 4:6

Jesus Christ taught that you would reap the results of your own thoughts, words, and actions. Therefore, you must learn to begin right each morning by connecting with God. Your connection with God is strengthened when you become still and silent in His peaceful presence. When you awake in the morning, spend time in communion with Him. Resist the temptation to rush into your morning, and instead discipline yourself to prioritize time with God. Your desire to be happy, prosperous, and of service to the world is contingent upon your ability to *seek first the Kingdom of God*.[90]

JUNE 11

"Rejoice in the Lord always. I will say it again: Rejoice!"
— Philippians 4:4

God wants you to experience the feeling sensations of happiness, peacefulness, joy, and prosperity. Sometimes in your life, the temptation to feel anxiety is great, and requires immense faith to overcome. However, this is the very faith God is challenging you to display: *To rejoice in the Lord always* — independent of the circumstances or conditions of your life. In other words, *do not be anxious about anything!* When the feelings of unease arise, simply refocus your attention on the presence of God. Immediately praise His name, and thank Him for the love and security that only He can provide. As you praise God in the midst of challenging times, your relationship and trust in Him is strengthened. Loving God when things are good is easy. To love God during trouble requires a heart like Jesus Christ.

JUNE 12

"I will extol the LORD at all times.
His praise will always be on my lips."

— Psalms 34:1

To develop a heart like Jesus Christ, you must first discipline yourself to think like Christ. By conditioning yourself to see the good in all the conditions of your life, you gradually move the direction of your life towards the good. Similarly, as you begin to lift the quality of your thoughts towards the good, you will begin to attract conditions, experiences, opportunities, people, attainments, and powers, which further express your ability to see what is good.[91] Regardless of the conditions of your life, goodness is always present, because God's presence is always with you. Instead of relying on external conditions to determine your emotional state, turn your attention inward and feel God's eternal love. God is always the same, and His love for you is always available.

JUNE 13

*"But the Lord is faithful, and he will strengthen
you and protect you from the evil one."*
— 2 Thessalonians 3:3

You do not have to do anything to receive God's peace. Nothing you do, or fail to do, will influence God's enduring love for you. This concept of *unconditional love* is beyond human understanding or application. In the world, you base your likes and dislikes upon conditions that either meet or fail your expectations. However, God's love for you is without condition. He loves you in the midst of what you consider a failure, just as much as He loves you during the joy of what you consider a success. Therefore, approach each day with a gentle confidence that *everything you say and do will prosper.*[92] Have faith that God is holding you in the palm of His hand, and is whispering words of encouragement. When you fall, He will lift you up. *He will soar you on wings of an eagle.*[93]

JUNE 14

"For everything God created is good, and nothing is to be rejected if it is received with thanksgiving, because it is consecrated by the Word of God and prayer."

— 1 Timothy 4-4:5

Continually lift your eyes to God. When your mind wanders during the day, return your awareness to God's presence. Because God is always by your side, even the briefest glance in His direction can reconnect you to His loving embrace. It is easy to feel isolated and alone, even in the midst of a large crowd. However, when you bask in the presence of God, you will feel secure and comforted, even when physically alone. When you learn to carry the presence of God with you throughout the day, you are doubly blessed: You receive God's grace, and you become a living channel of God's peace to others.

JUNE 15

"The lions may grow weak and hungry, but those who seek the Lord will lack no good thing."

— Psalm 34:10

There are many lessons to be gathered from Jesus Christ's teaching of *reaping what you sow*. The imagery of the farmer reaping the benefits of his harvest uncovers one of the more challenging aspects of what God longs for you to understand. After the farmer sowed the seeds of his crop, he endured a long season of caring for the soil. A great deal of time passed, and when the season was just right, the seeds flourished, and he reaped the bountiful harvest. Oftentimes, you forget about the nature of time, and become frustrated when things do not go according to your plan. However, everything is always going according to plan, because God's plans for you are divinely orchestrated. Every seed you plant will provide a harvest for you, according to God's perfect timing. Your primary role in the creative process is to plant. God's primary role in the creative process is to provide.

JUNE 16

"For the LORD God is a sun and shield; The LORD gives grace and glory; No good thing does He withhold from those who walk uprightly."

— Psalm 84:11-12

Any thought, word, or action repeated over time will become a habit. A fully-formed habit in your life can be so powerful that decisions are made without conscious awareness. This is the reason stillness and silence in the presence of God is so important for you. When you become still in the loving embrace of God, His grace will lift you up from the depths of negativity and limited patterns of thinking that no longer serve you. In the light of His mercy, deep-rooted thoughts of self-doubt, insecurity, and fear will melt away. Your mind will be like an empty cup, ready to receive the glorious supply of faith, hope, love, positivity, and encouragement that God longs to provide.

JUNE 17

"Therefore I tell you, whatever you ask for in prayer, believe that you have received it, and it will be yours."

— Mark 11:24

An old wise farmer had just returned home from the laborious task of toiling the soil, and planting the seed. A long day's work behind him, the farmer felt gratitude for the harvest his seeds would surely provide.

The farmer's young son approached him and asked,

"Father, can we go check on the seeds tomorrow to see if they've grown?"

"How will we determine if they have grown?" the farmer asked.

"We will dig them up, and see if they have sprouted!" the son excitedly replied.

"If we dig up the seeds, they will surely perish, for their time has not come for harvest. We must wait for the season, and have faith in what our eyes cannot see," the wise farmer said.

JUNE 18

"You shall fear only the LORD your God; and you shall worship Him and swear by His name. You shall not follow other gods, any of the gods of the peoples who surround you."

— Deuteronomy 6:13-14

God is desirous of your praise, worship, and undivided attention. Whatever thoughts occupy your mind the majority of the time will become your god. Worry and anxiety, if indulged and focused upon, take up a life of their own, skewing your perspective of circumstances, people, and situations. You must develop the willpower to break free of the bondage of self-imposed idolatry by continually returning your attention to God. Although what goes on in your mind is invisible to other people, God is able to read your thoughts, and He is searching for evidence of devotion to Him. Therefore, abide by these precious words of Jesus Christ: *Love the Lord your God with all your heart and with all your soul and with all your mind and with all your strength.*

JUNE 19

"Ascribe to the LORD, Oh sons of the mighty; Ascribe to the LORD glory and strength. Ascribe to the LORD the glory due to His name; Worship the LORD in holy array."

— Psalm 29-1:2

When you worship and praise God, take a moment to include the senses of your eyes, ears, and hands. Today, write down your favorite Bible verse, and then read the verse out loud several times. Do you recall the feelings once attained from writing a love letter to a husband, wife, or a loved one? The passion, excitement, and positive expectancy gained from the act of writing the letter was immense. In this same fashion, God is desirous of your passion, excitement, and positive expectancy. When you take time from your busy schedule to write the Word of God, and then read it, and speak it, the power of His Word is significantly awakened in your heart and mind.

JUNE 20

"But an hour is coming, and now is, when the true worshipers will worship the Father in spirit and truth; for such people the Father seeks to be His worshipers."

— John 4:23

You have developed a keen sense of time. You tend to base decisions of priority on the amount of time they will take. However, you serve a God who lives in timelessness: *Jesus Christ is the same yesterday, today, and forever.*[94] Although you are bound by time, God can transcend the twenty-four hours of your day. God is desirous of your continual awareness, not a segmented allotment of your time. Develop the ability to hold the presence of God in your awareness throughout every moment of your day. Allow the face of God to continually shine upon you, giving you peace and serenity.

JUNE 21

"I am the vine; you are the branches. If you remain in me and I in you, you will bear much fruit."

— John 15:5

God has awareness of your thoughts, words, and actions. He sees everything without judgment, but instead with compassion and forgiveness. When you realize that the presence of God is within you, and watching over you, then everything will begin to change. Because the conditions of your life are in direct proportion to your own thinking, and God is aware of your thoughts, you must condition yourself to think positively. When you notice the downward pull of negative self-talk has taken hold of your mind, whisper out loud, *"Help me, God."* Then take a deep breath, and experience His presence. When you welcome God's embrace, you surrender into His loving arms all degrees of negativity. God will fill your mind with grace and mercy, and lift your spirit to a heavenly realm.

JUNE 22

*"Accompanied by trumpets, cymbals and
other instruments, the singers raised their voices
in praise to the LORD and sang:
'He is good; His love endures forever.'"*

— 2 Chronicles 5:13

God is asking you to follow Him one step at a time through the great adventures of your life. The challenge you face is to remain focused on the path God is currently leading you, instead of looking at the mountains looming in the future. When you look too far into the future, anxiety easily overcomes you, and it is far too easy to miss golden opportunities that are standing directly in front of you. When you remember that God will equip you with everything you need at the exact time and place you need it, remaining focused on the path you are on today becomes much easier. Trust that when you are actually standing directly before the mountain, God will show you a safe path and help you scale the heights. He will perfectly equip you for the climb, and hold your hand every step of the way.

JUNE 23

"Finally, be strong in the Lord and in his mighty power. Put on the full armor of God, so that you can take your stand against the devil's schemes."

— Ephesians 6:10-12

Today, allow God to be your strength and shield. Trust that God has this day planned out for you, and everything in His plan is for your good. Instead of worrying what is on the road ahead of you today, focus your energy on remaining in contact with God. *When you seek God first, everything else is provided for you.*[95] The energy associated with worry, anxiety, and fear is immense, and easily drains you of creative potential. Therefore, cast off these negative emotions, and focus your mind only upon what is *good, wonderful, and righteous.* Entrust yourself to the mighty protective armor of God, and have faith *He is with you wherever you go.*

JUNE 24

"Let the peace of Christ rule in your hearts, since as members of one body you were called to peace."

— Colossians 3:15

When it rains heavily for several days, and the water remains on the surface of the earth for an extended period of time, the water begins to seep deep into the soil, allowing for life and growth to take place. This is the same manner in which God's love can seep into your mind when you spend long periods of time in His presence.[96] Therefore, become still in God's presence so that His love may flow freely through you. Just like any skill, you can train your mind to remain focused on God. When you observe the habits of your mind, you will notice they tend to advance far into the future, and get snagged on a mind-created problem. When you notice your mind has left the serenity of the present moment, simply return awareness to your breath, and whisper God's Holy name. When you are fully awake in the present moment, God's mercy and grace will envelop you. His face will shine both within you, and over you, and *goodness will surely follow you all the days of your life.*[97]

JUNE 25

*"He who dwells in the shelter of the Most High
will rest in the shadow of the Almighty."*

— Psalm 91:1

You live in a world that associates accomplishment with physically doing something. This social conditioning creates anxiety, and a felt need to be checking things off a to-do list. In the world, this mistaken means of prioritizing success can be extremely alluring. However, in God's Kingdom, success and accomplishment are achieved not in the act of doing more, but rather in the sacrifice of doing less. God is desirous of your time, your stillness, and your worship. Although quieting your mind and stilling your body is somewhat challenging for you, the ability to develop these skills is immensely valuable during the great adventures of your life. In stillness, God is able to replenish your energy, and lift heavy-laden burdens from your shoulders. *Dwell in the peace of the Lord.*

JUNE 26

"Be still, and know that I am God."

— Psalm 46:10

In Hebrew, the word *"Raphah"* means to *"be still, to sink and to relax."* Consider this ancient translation in the context of *being "raphah" in the presence of the Lord*. God is desirous of more than your ability to simply make your body still. God wants you to physically sink into His mighty embrace, and relax your mind in the peaceful nature of His love. Learning to completely relax in the presence of God is a display of your confident trust in His ability to provide all your needs. Become one with the rock of God, and allow His strong qualities to resonate throughout your entire being.

JUNE 27

*"But when you pray, go into your room,
close the door and pray to your Father, who
is unseen. Then your Father, who sees what
is done in secret, will reward you."*

— Matthew 6:6

There are many people, commitments, and sensory objects that compete for your attention. You live in a world where the concept of "multi-tasking" is a valued skill, allowing you to accomplish multiple things at the same time. In the material world, completing tasks simultaneously may serve you. However, in order to seek the Kingdom of God, you must discipline yourself to focus exclusively upon His peaceful presence. Only when you remove all other sensory distractions from your awareness can you begin to fully experience the presence of God within you. This is what Jesus Christ meant when he said *"Go into your room, and close the door."* When the eyes are closed and the body becomes still, your mind will gradually come to a resting point at the feet of God. His love and light will radiate within you, and your devotion will be rewarded by His grace and mercy.

JUNE 28

*"He reveals deep and hidden things; He knows
what lies in darkness and light dwells with Him."*
— Daniel 2:22

God sees everything and is completely aware of *what you do in
secret.* Many people live under the false pretense their thoughts
are their private affair. However, nothing could be further from the
truth. God is aware of your every thought, word, and action. To live
with *integrity* means your ability to abide by certain principles,
even in the privacy of your own home, and the intimacy of your
own mind. Principles of righteous thinking, speaking, and action
are like Northern stars, guiding you to the ultimate destination of
your soul. Even in the privacy of your mind-temple, you must ensure good-natured thinking is the cosmic vibration you are projecting into God's Universe.

JUNE 29

"Praise be to the God and Father of our LORD Jesus Christ, who has blessed us in the heavenly realms with every spiritual blessing in Christ."

— Ephesians 1:3

The temptation of procrastination is a force of great power in the world. This dark and engulfing illusion of postponement often comes between you and God's presence. You tend to prioritize what will bring immediate pleasure over what will provide lasting value. Time with God is the greatest investment you can make, providing you with both immediate benefit and long term reward. Every moment spent in the presence of God blesses you richly, overflowing your spirit with peace. The excess is stored up for you, with compounding interest doubling the initial investment of your time. Do not put off your ability to experience God until tomorrow. God is within you, and hovering over you, in this very moment. Open your heart, open your mind, and open your arms to His loving embrace. *Rejoice always, pray continually, and give thanks in all circumstances.*[98]

JUNE 30

"Humble yourself, therefore, under God's mighty hand, that He may lift you up in due time."

— 1 Peter 5:6

Although you can choose to follow any path during the great adventures of your life, only one path was made just for you. You have unique talents, and ways of expressing your divine gifts that God intended exclusively for you. These talents and gifts are for your benefit, and the benefit of everyone you come into contact with. When you shine the great light within you, God magnifies the intensity of your power. Do not let anyone or anything dim your light, or convince you to follow a path you feel distant from. Hold tightly to the hand of God, and allow His leadership to guide your thoughts and actions. You were divinely created for goodness, for justice, and to joyfully express the great heart within you.

JULY

"As for God, His way is perfect; the Word of the LORD is flawless. He is a shield for all who take refuge in Him."

— 2 Samuel 22:31

JULY 1

"For God so loved the world, that He gave His only Son, that whoever believes in Him should not perish but have eternal life."

— John 3:16

God loves you with an everlasting, steady, secure, permanent, and unconditional love. Although your mind stretches to understand the magnitude of unconditional love, the true application in worldly relationships is beyond your capacity to provide, or receive. Your emotions are like the ebb and flow of the sea, varying with the circumstances and conditions of your life. Even the love you give and receive in the most intimate relationships is in continual flux. Only God is capable of providing you the permanent love and steadiness of relationship you so desperately desire and need. Your longing for God's love and His love for you are a perfect match.

JULY 2

"Humble yourselves, therefore, under the mighty hand of God so that at the proper time He may exalt you, casting all your anxieties on Him, because He cares for you."

— 1 Peter 5:6-7

Rejoice in this day that God has made. Trust that God is alive and abundantly present within you and all around you, and prepare yourself to receive His blessings. When you completely surrender to God's embrace, you release all worry into His care. The space within your mind that was holding the energy of anxiety and uncertainty then opens to the gifts God has stored up for you. To seek God's Kingdom requires active participation on your part, the primary task being the removal of all clutter and hindrances to His presence. The majority of what is preventing you from completely receiving the warmth of God's embrace is your own limited thinking. Live first and foremost for God. Walk with God always in your heart, and on your mind. The path God has set before you is full of abundant life and peace.

JULY 3

*"So, leaving them again, He went away and prayed
for the third time, saying the same words again."*
— Matthew 26:44

You have developed the ability to become physically still and silent in the presence of God. The next step is to learn to control your mind. Your mind has the ability to create internal turmoil and unease. Even in worldly paradise, your mind can perceive darkness. In order to fill your mind with God's light, you must surrender your thinking to Him. One way to accomplish this is to repeat God's Word over and over in your mind. Repetition is the first law of learning. Everything you have learned to do, from walking to talking, was achieved through repetition. Therefore, discipline yourself to repeat God's Word. When your mind is rebelling, take a deep breath and speak His Word out loud. Then close your eyes, and repeat the same verse several more times within the temple of your mind and spirit. *The prayer of a righteous person has great power as it is working.*[99]

JULY 4

"After the earthquake came a fire, but the Lord was not in the fire. And after the fire came a gentle whisper."

— 1 Kings 19:12

Remember that God is always with you. He is in the midst of your most challenging circumstances. He is beside you during the most joyful times. God is continually within you, and always steadfast beside you. Your challenge is to resonate with God, and to experience His peace during the ebb and flow of life. From the energetic center of peace, your challenging circumstances loose their sharp edge. From the perspective of peace, you recognize God as the provider of all good things. Therefore, regardless of what you might be experiencing in any given moment, remember the words of Jesus Christ and have faith: *"Take courage. It is I."*[100]

JULY 5

*"You will seek me and find me, when you
search for me with all your heart."*
— Jeremiah 29:13

You will seek and find God, when you search for Him with all your mind and heart. Jesus Christ promised that whatsoever you earnestly sought, you would find. Whatever you asked for, you would receive. Whatever door you knocked upon would be opened before you. Your role in God's Universe, therefore, is to prepare yourself to receive His promises. In addition, once a joyful gift has been received, your job is to be grateful to the *giver of the gift*, who is always greater than the gift you have received. Everything you experience in the world will come and go. Clinging to artifacts of the world leads to suffering. Holding tightly to the hand of God leads to abounding happiness and peace.

JULY 6

"His name will be called Wonderful Counselor,
Mighty God, Everlasting Father, Prince of Peace."

— Isaiah 9:6

God wants to know about every intimate detail of your life. You are aware of God's promises, and understand conceptually that God is always with you. However, to understand with the mind and to understand with the heart are two different things. The habit of your mind is to seek control of your circumstances. Your heart longs to surrender circumstances to God. Your mind tends to bounce from one thought to another. Your heart desires rest in the pasture of the Lord. Your mind projects itself into the past and future. Your heart is perfectly content in the immediate moment. As you experience the great adventures of this day, lead from your heart. *Delight yourself in the Lord, and He will give you the desires of your heart.*[101]

JULY 7

"You are my lamp, O LORD; the LORD
turns my darkness into light."

— 2 Samuel 22:29

God has the ability to turn darkness into light. Because God is the Light of the world, He can illuminate and brighten the darkest and coldest corners of your heart. When you feel the world is weighing heavily upon your shoulders, remember that the presence of God is within you, and that Jesus Christ overcame the world. In any given moment of your life, you have a critical choice to make: You can either focus on the world, or the One who overcame it. As you learn to redirect your awareness to God's light, He will gently push back the darkness, and help guide your thoughts to peaceful pastures. To walk along God's path is the greatest joy in your life.

JULY 8

"Speak to one another with psalms, hymns and spiritual songs. Sing and make music in your heart to the LORD, always giving thanks to God the Father for everything, in the name of our Lord Jesus Christ."
— Ephesians 5:19-20

Your body tends to go the direction your eyes are looking. In athletic endeavors such as skiing, a wise coach will direct an athlete to look into the turn, even though the athlete might be accelerating in the other direction. If the athlete can trust their coach, and keep their eyes focused on the direction they want to go, their body will surely follow. This lesson applies to both the eyes within your head and the eyes within your heart. Whatever you are looking at, focusing upon and thinking about will become stronger and more prevalent in your life. Your life will turn the direction of both your eyes and heart. Therefore, keep your eyes and your heart focused upon the Lord.

JULY 9

"Then Jesus spoke to them again, saying, 'I am the light of the world. He who follows me shall not walk in darkness, but have the light of life.'"

— John 8:12

There are three distinct ways to experience prayer. In the first method, your mind focuses on God for a few moments, then becomes distracted and drifts away. Through the use of willpower, your mind regains focus upon God. In the second method, your mind remains undisturbed and focused upon God. In the third method, you and God become One. The first method gradually leads to the second. Through the silence, peace and stillness of the second method of prayer, the third will effortlessly arise within your heart. In the bliss of the third method of prayer, you will gain an understanding of Jesus Christ's proclamation, *"My Father and I are One."*[102]

JULY 10

"Our light and momentary troubles are achieving for us an eternal glory that far outweighs them all."

— 2 Corinthians 4:17

When you become still and silent in the presence of God, your mind takes on the quality of a pristine body of water. Your mind becomes stable, and the sediment normally held in suspension that clouds your thinking sinks to the bottom, allowing for a brilliant clarity. It is through acute awareness of God that you cultivate the ability to think, speak, and act with divinity and holiness. The primary tool at your disposal is your breathing. When you create a momentary pause before responding to any internal or external stimulus, you allow space for cognitive reflection, prayer, and right action. It is the momentary pause in the process of cause and effect that allows God to free you from the bondage of habitual patterns of reaction.

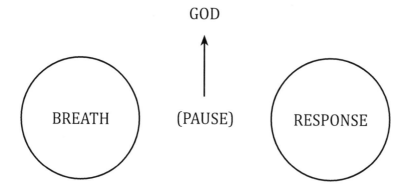

GOD

BREATH (PAUSE) RESPONSE

JULY 11

*"He is able to save forever those who
draw near to God through him."*

— Hebrews 7:25

No rising thought wave can escape the presence of God. Because the presence of God is within you, He is also aware of you, and capable of knowing your every thought. When you cultivate stillness in your mind, a great space opens within you, and your awareness of God expands into it. The process of expanding into God's presence eventually leads to the bending of worldly time as you currently comprehend it. Instead of being caught up in the movement of time as an inescapable current, you enjoy it as a series of discrete and present moments, all held in the hand of God. Great athletes possess this quality at the level of the body's intelligence. They seem to move in slow motion, while simultaneously running circles around their opponents. They can effortlessly dominate as they please. Stillness, prayer, and silence will create the same effect in every corner of your life experience.

JULY 12

"I will greatly rejoice in the LORD, my soul shall be joyful in my God; for He has clothed me with the garments of salvation, He has covered me with the robe of righteousness."

— Isaiah 61:10

Trust God enough to spend generous amounts of time with Him. As you develop the discipline to *seek first the Kingdom of God,*[103] you will happily discover that in His Kingdom, peacefulness abides. The details of your life are in the hands of God. When you really surrender to this fact, you are immediately free from the self-imposed chains for the desire to control. Attempting to control the future is a waste of precious life-energy. Rather than directing your mind and energy into the illusion of controlling future events, pull back on the reigns of your thinking, and become still in the presence of God. *Let tomorrow worry about tomorrow.*[104] *Rejoice greatly in the presence of God.*

JULY 13

*"Every word of God is flawless; He is a shield
to those who take refuge in Him."*
— Proverbs 30:5

God wants to be both your sword and shield. In the warrior tradition, the symbols of the sword and shield hold immense significance. The shield was used by the warrior not as a means of personal protection, but to protect the warrior's fellow comrades. Similarly, God wants to use His mighty shield to protect you, and keep you from harm. However, you must take the active step of seeking shelter behind His protective armor. You have a tendency to wander outside of God's guardianship, and to struggle against the current of life's great ocean. When you have the discipline to remain in His watch-care, you gain a better perspective of your circumstances. From the safe zone established behind God's loving shield, you have time to experience His presence, and receive His guidance in your decision-making. *Allow God to be your refuge and protection.*

JULY 14

"You will keep him in perfect peace, whose mind is stayed on You, because he trusts in You."

— Isaiah 26:3

You must learn to discern the difference between the areas of your life that are of concern to you, and the areas of your life you can actually influence. You tend to spend a great deal of time and energy worrying about things that are out of your control. Meanwhile, the parts of your life that you can do something about remain neglected, only compounding the anxiety you feel over what you cannot control. When you discover unease or worry has infiltrated your thinking, release the situation into the loving hands of God. Trust that God will provide everything you need, according to His perfect timing. Then redirect your mind to the area of your life you always retain dominion over, which is your thinking. The quality of your thinking will always be in direct proportion to the quality of your life experience.

JULY 15

*"Trust in the LORD with all your heart and
lean not on your own understanding."*

— Proverbs 3:5

God wants to be your spiritual compass. When you allow God to influence the direction of your life, the journey becomes much more enjoyable. Rather than leaning on your own understanding, trust that God is leading you to a destination of great reward. As Jesus Christ directed his disciples, *"Follow me."*

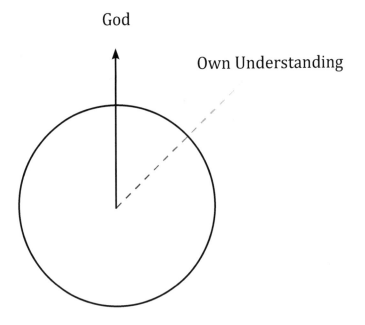

JULY 16

"He put a new song in my mouth, a hymn of praise to our God. Many will see and fear and put their trust in the LORD."

— Psalm 40:3

Watching the flow of your breath will assist your mind in becoming still. Furthermore, your concentration will be strengthened, ultimately enhancing your ability to focus solely on God. The power of your concentration will allow you to invest your life energy in communion with God. The gift of your breath is the gift of life, bestowed upon you by God, the Creator of the Universe. Every time you inhale, you are receiving His grace and mercy. Each breath is co-created between you and God, and should be experienced with gratitude, reverence, and love. Allow every inhalation to be long, subtle, deep, rhythmic, and evenly spread throughout your entire body. By pausing briefly at the top of the breath, the mind will become tranquil, and a sensation of lightness will envelop you. Because breath is life, the art of mindful breathing is an opportunity for you to create space between your thoughts. Within this space, the presence of God will welcome you home.

JULY 17

"We do not lose heart. Though our outer self is wasting away, our inner self is being renewed day by day."

— 2 Corinthians 4:16

The presence of God is within you. Therefore, in order to experience His presence, you must learn to turn your attention inward. When you become still, and close your eyes, the normal pull of external sensation and gratification is reduced. Physical stillness and silence is the beginning of the withdrawal from the external engagement of the mind and senses. With body still and eyes closed, you can focus on the feelings and sensations within your heart. No matter how hard you might try, you cannot look into your mind or heart with your eyes. Instead, you must cultivate the ability to feel the rise and fall of emotion, wisdom, and intuition. This ability is achieved by surrendering to the mighty power of God. You cannot catch a wild horse in the field by chasing after it. However, if you stand still and hold out an apple, the wild horse will eventually come to you.

JULY 18

"Blessed are those who have learned to acclaim you,
who walk in the light of your presence, Oh LORD."

— Psalm 89:15

A great skill that you can cultivate is the ability to witness your own thinking. When you become still in the presence of God, you will learn to watch the emergence of your own thoughts. This watching-self is your witness; it is the Holy Spirit, alive and well within you. As you witness the rise and fall of thoughts, your higher self, through the power of the Holy Spirit, can nip negativity in the bud before it occupies your mind. The calmness and peacefulness achieved through this practice will allow for divine consciousness, where you and God merge as One. To summarize, the three steps of the daily discipline are as follows:

1. Become still.

2. Witness the space between your thoughts.

3. Experience the presence of God.

JULY 19

"Thus says the LORD of hosts, 'Return to Me,' declares the LORD of hosts, 'That I may return to you,' says the LORD."

— Zachariah 1:3

The sensations in your body are like a compass either directing you closer to, or further away from, the presence of God. Any sensation of comfort or peacefulness is your internal compass pointing you towards God. Sensations of discomfort or anxiety are a warning you are moving further away from God. Experiencing the presence of God is therefore a matter of turning the attention inward, and developing sensitivity to the feelings within your heart. God is always within you, and alongside you. His promise is to never leave or forsake you. Therefore, when you feel unease, fear, anxiety, or worry, take heart that God is still there, eagerly awaiting your return. *Return to the Lord, your God, so that He may return to you.*

JULY 20

"I will give them a heart to know me, for I am the LORD."
— Jeremiah 24:7

In the Bible it says, *"Be still, and know that I am God."*[105] Stillness is the first requirement to experience the presence of God. In the stillness of God's presence, you connect with His Universe, and become One with the Creator. Although it goes against the grain of worldly advice, in God's presence, you can actually *do less and accomplish more.* This is why Jesus Christ taught his disciples to *"Seek first the Kingdom of God, and everything else will be added to you."*[106] Imagine throwing a little pebble into a still body of water, and watching the ripple effect created by the stone's slight impulse. Then, when the water returns to stillness, you gently introduce another small pebble. This is exactly what happens when you experience the presence of God. Any prayer or heartfelt intention introduced into God's Universe will ripple across the great adventure of your life. The first step, therefore, is to directly experience His Universe, and this is achieved through silence, stillness, and prayer.

JULY 21

*"Then you should return to Me. And if
you will put away your detested things
from My presence, I will not waver."*

— Jeremiah 4:1

When you are experiencing yourself as your own thinking, you severely impact your ability to experience God. One of the giant leaps of consciousness God is desirous for you to achieve is your ability to understand you are not your thoughts. When you are constantly judging, labeling, worrying, and internally struggling, you are restricting the flow of energy between you and God. Contrast this with the ability to create simultaneous internal stillness and expansiveness, and you will begin to understand why God instructs you to become *still in His presence*.[107] When you are still, you take on the qualities of a pristine mirror, and are able to reflect God's presence within you to the world around you. Even as you move through the great adventure of your day, remain in communion with the *still small voice* within you.[108] *Put away detested things, and return to His presence.*

JULY 22

"The angel of the LORD encamps all around those who fear Him, and delivers them."

— Psalm 34:6

God knows you far better than you will ever know yourself. God has compassion for your uniqueness, your complexity, and your talents. *No detail of your life is hidden from God.*[109] *He is even aware of your thoughts.*[110] Instead of fearing His presence, invite His grace and mercy into your awareness. God knows you; the purpose of your life is to get to know God. Spending time with God is like priming the pump of a well. At first, your willpower is needed to become still and silent in His presence. However, as you continue to bring God the sacrifice of your time, His spirit is able to expand within you. Your direct experience of God's grace and mercy will produce deeper levels of communion, until you are overflowing with God's love.

JULY 23

"For the LORD has said, 'I am concerned for you, and will look on you with favor.'"

— Exodus 4:31

Worry acts on your mind like a great storm acts upon the ocean. The surface contents of the sea are whirled and churned up, creating treacherous conditions. Similarly, negativity churns up your mind, creating conditions in your life that ultimately lead to more worry, anxiety, and concern. Worry casts a dark shadow over your entire life, a shadow that God longs to penetrate through the light of His love. God is in a position to see the conditions of tomorrow more clearly than you can even remember the events that took place yesterday. Therefore, rest easy in His embrace, trusting your future into His capable hands.

JULY 24

*"Commit to the LORD whatever you do,
and your plans will succeed."*

— Proverbs 16:3

Look to God continually for support, encouragement, and companionship. Even the slightest glance in His direction can reconnect you with His loving embrace. God's power always flows freely from His presence. Therefore, when you are able to reside in His presence, you simultaneously reside in His power. Your recognition of God's presence, in both large and small matters, grants you unlimited access to His strength, power, and love. This is why in the Bible it says: *"You shall do all things through Christ, who strengthens you."*[111] You never have to face a challenge alone. Any obstacle set out before you can be surmounted with God.

JULY 25

"God did not give us a spirit of timidity, but a spirit of power, of love, and self-discipline."
— 2 Timothy 1:7

To navigate the world successfully, you must abide by Law as created and enforced by man. Similarly, to navigate God's Universe successfully, you must abide by His Law, or suffer from the consequences of ignorance. There are no exceptions within God's Law. Although His love for you is great, He also granted you free will, which you can use to break both God's Law and man's law. One of the greatest Laws as taught by Jesus Christ was forgiveness. When you hold onto anger, frustration, or resentment, you allow for the seeds of the emotion to continue to manifest in your life. However, when you forgive any emotion or condition of negativity, you allow for the equal and opposite condition to arise. Forgiving anger creates space for happiness. Forgiving poverty allows space for the creation of wealth. Forgiving brokenness allows space for God's peace to lovingly embrace your heart.

JULY 26

*"Be strong and courageous. Do not be afraid
or terrified, for the LORD our God goes with
you; He will never leave or forsake you."*
— Deuteronomy 31:6

The main cause of negativity in your life arises from feelings of anger, fear, greed, and unhealthy competition. These stress-producing feelings create a draining effect on your mind, soul, and body. In contrast, the positive feelings of love, cooperation, courage, and faith produce an uplifting and energizing effect. Jesus Christ taught that darkness could never cast out darkness. Only through the presence of God's love can darkness be turned into light. Therefore, when you are experiencing the rise of negative emotions, simply become still in the presence of God. Breathe deeply and evenly, allowing each exhale to release tension from your body. Because your mind and body are so intimately connected, releasing tension from your body will produce a similar effect in your mind. With the body still and the mind calm, God's presence will cast out any darkness within you. His love and light will shine within you, through you, and all around you.

JULY 27

*"Ask where the good way is, and walk in it,
and you will find rest for your souls."*

— Jeremiah 6:16

An old wise man stood before the gates of an ancient city. A disgruntled traveler approached the old man and asked,

"What kind of people live in this city?"

The old man replied, *"What kind of people were in the city from whence you came?"*

"Oh, they were cruel, mean, and negative," the traveler said.

"You will find those same people in this city," the old man sighed.

Later in the day, a young and kindhearted traveler approached the old man, inquiring about the people in the city.

"What kind of people live in this city," asked the traveler.

The old man replied, *"What kind of people were in the city from whence you came?"*

"Oh, they were kind, loving, and very positive," the traveler said.

The old man happily responded, *"You will find those same people in this city."*

JULY 28

"The Kingdom of God cometh not with observation: Neither shall they say, 'Look here' or 'Look there' for behold, the Kingdom of God is within you."

— Luke 17:20-21

God's Kingdom is within you. Your soul is a reflection of God's immortal soul, and when you experience His presence, you will encompass God's infinite capacity for love, peace, and wisdom. Jesus Christ's teachings on God's Kingdom were at the heart of his message. From the very beginning of Christ's public ministry, the Bible records that *"Christ came into Galilee, preaching the gospel of the Kingdom of God."*[112] The only prayer Christ gave his disciples beseeches God, *"Thy Kingdom come."*[113] God's Kingdom is not to be discovered by visual observation or through the stimuli-tuned senses of hearing, taste, smell, or touch. Instead, you must learn to turn your attention inward, and to interiorize the presence of God, who is already within you.

JULY 29

*"I form light and create darkness, I make
well-being and create calamity, I am the
LORD, who does all these things."*
— Isaiah 45:7

God is the source of supply for everything your heart desires. Therefore, in the creative process, *believing always precedes achieving.* Concepts of lack, limitation, and poverty are an illusion of your mind, and tend to come from your habit of external object identification. As long as you search for fulfillment in object referral, you will remain unhappy. You were hard-wired for God-connection since birth, and the search for God is often mistaken by your senses as a need for external gratification. Only by turning your attention inward and searching inside yourself, will you discover that God has been waiting for you the entire time.

JULY 30

"In the beginning, God created the Heavens and the earth. The earth was without form and void, and darkness was over the face of the deep. And the Spirit of God was hovering over the face of the waters. And God said, 'Let there be light,' and there was light."

— Genesis 1:1

In God's Universe, there is only infinite abundance and perpetual prosperity. God has absolutely no concept of lack, for He is the Divine Creator of all things, both seen and unseen. You must embrace your birthright as a creator, and join God in the creative process, which is His intention for you. You were made in the image of God, and are both a creation and a creator. Therefore, you must develop your ability to focus on *what you desire*. When the desires of your heart are formed and held clearly in your mind, God will always provide for the fulfillment of your intention or something even greater. *Your God supplies all your need, according to His riches, in the Glory of Christ Jesus.*[114]

JULY 31

"And he called the twelve together and gave them power and authority over all demons and to cure diseases, and he sent them out to proclaim the Kingdom of God and to heal."

— Luke 9:1

In this very moment, every desire of your heart exists as formless energetic potential in God's Universe. Therefore, it is never a matter of getting what you want; it is simply a matter of receiving what you already have. This is accomplished in three ways:

1. Seek first the Kingdom of God.

2. Focus on what you desire, not the lack of it.

3. Praise God for His ability to provide all your needs.

When your thoughts, words, emotions, and actions are in harmony with God, the desires of your heart will be effortlessly placed at your feet. *Seek first God's Kingdom, and everything else will be given to you.*[115]

AUGUST

"Humble yourselves under the mighty hand of God, that He may exalt you in due time, casting all your care upon Him, for He cares for you."

— 1 Peter 5:6-7

AUGUST 1

"The LORD is my rock, my fortress and my deliverer; my God is my rock, in whom I take refuge, my shield and the horn of my salvation. He is my stronghold, my refuge and my savior—from violent men you save me."

— 2 Samuel 22:1-3

When you spend time focusing on yourself, you experience ever-increasing amounts of worry. When you spend time focusing on God, you experience ever-increasing amounts of joy. Worry is the result of your limited creative thinking. When you focus on yourself, you essentially squeeze the space for God out of your awareness. Worry therefore results, because you feel isolated, alone, and unsupported. When you spend time thinking about God, you naturally invite His ever-present love into your awareness. His presence uplifts you, because you realize you are not alone. Therefore, it is not a matter of thinking *less of yourself.* It is simply a shift in perspective to thinking *about yourself less, and more about God.*

AUGUST 2

"I will give you the keys of the kindgom of heaven."
— Matthew 16:19

The concept of a master key has always been a topic of fascination to locksmiths. The notion that one master key could unlock an infinity of secured doors captures one's imagination and sense of adventure. God desperately wants you to realize that He is that very key which can unlock the door to your heart's greatest desires. God is the master key of your life. Only a mind and heart focused on God can unravel the mysteries of the universe. When you earnestly search for God with all your heart, all your mind, and all your soul, you will find Him. In the moment of discovery, God will unveil to you the key to your greatest hopes, dreams, and aspirations. The golden key God desires to place in your hand will most importantly allow you access to the gates of Heaven.

AUGUST 3

"If anyone speaks, he should do it as one speaking the very Words of God. If anyone serves, he should do it with the strength God provides, so that in all things God may be praised through Jesus Christ. To him be the glory and the power for ever and ever."

— 1 Peter 4:11

There is a small space between every thought that passes across the screen of your consciousness, and your reaction to it. In this space is the peace of God. With practice, you can learn to instantly discern the difference between your habitual patterns of thinking, and inspired thoughts directly from God. As you become still in God's presence, His presence within you will begin to expand. You will notice His influence on your thinking in critical moments. The stillness you cultivate through meditation on His presence will carry over into your daily life experience, *and His goodness will follow you all the days of your life.*[116]

AUGUST 4

"The LORD is my strength and my defense; He has become my salvation. He is my God, and I will praise Him."

— Exodus 15:2

God is calling you to have a heart and mind like His Son, Jesus Christ. Your birthright as a son or daughter of God is a natural state of health, radiant wellness, strength, resilience, and abundance. The only thing preventing you from abiding within this natural state of divine perfection is your own wrong thinking. Having a heart like Christ requires having a mind like Christ. You are only limited by self-imposed beliefs and ideals. God does not limit you—you limit yourself. When you embrace God with all your mind, all your soul, and all your heart, then God will embrace you. The very thoughts of God will begin to take up residence in your mind. Your life will be a living testimony of faith, grace, and mercy.

AUGUST 5

"Therefore I tell you, whatever you ask for in prayer, believe that you have received it, and it will be yours."

— Mark 11:24

There is a world of difference between thinking about *what you desire*, and thinking about the *method of its obtainment*. Your job in the creative process is to hold in your mind the image of what you desire. Leave the method of obtainment in the capable hands of God. When you focus on the means by which your desires are to be achieved, you severely limit yourself to the worldly strengths you currently possess. However, when you leave the method of receiving your requests up to God, you open the space for miracles and divine appointments to take place. Remember that when you pray to God, your primary purpose is to bring before Him the requests of your heart. Then praise Him with trust and faithfulness for the fulfillment of your desires, or something even greater than you can ask or imagine. You provide the desire; God provides the method of fulfillment.

AUGUST 6

"And the peace of God, which transcends all understanding, will guard your hearts and your minds in Christ Jesus."

— Philippians 4:7

A spiritually mature prayer is a heartfelt request for God to renew your mind. Because the quality of your thinking will always be reflected by the quality of your life, inviting God into your mind unlocks the potential for a higher perspective of every situation. A renewed mind takes on the qualities of a pristine body of water. From time to time, waves gently ripple across the surface; however, the depths of the water always remain still. With attention turned inward, you access the depths of your soul, which is where God's presence resides. By asking God to renew your mind, you actually begin to think less, and feel more. When thoughts do arise, instead of identifying with the thought as who you are, you witness the thoughts from your higher perspective. Your heart becomes your guide, leading you home to your authentic self and welcoming arms of God.

AUGUST 7

*"Then you will call on me and come and
pray to me, and I will listen to you."*

— Jeremiah 29:12

God takes great delight in you, and *rejoices over you with singing.*[117]
In the world, you will experience heartache, setback, and trouble.
However, in God you will only experience peace, grace, mercy,
abounding love, and enduring compassion. During the course of
your day, learn to take moments of silence to feel the presence of
God's embrace. These brief moments will become a refuge from
worldly pressure and demand, providing much needed nourishment for your spirit. God wants to reveal Himself to you, and your
seeking heart will rejoice in His splendor.

AUGUST 8

"Let us then approach God's throne of grace with confidence, so that we may receive mercy and find grace to help us in our time of need."

— Hebrews 4:16

God is calling you to have a heart like His Son, Jesus Christ. Courage, confidence, self-love, and self-esteem are emotions that God is desirous for you to experience on a regular basis. These feelings and emotions are substantiated not by your own strength, but by the strength of God, who is within you. To wallow in negativity, self-doubt, and insecurity is to deny God. Remember who you are, and more importantly, remember Who is with you. You are royalty, because you are a divine child of a Heavenly King. And God, your King and the Creator of the universe, of everything that is seen and unseen, loves you with all His heart. *Approach God with confidence, so that you may receive help in your time of need.*

AUGUST 9

"But when you ask, you must believe and not doubt, because the one who doubts is like a wave of the sea, blown and tossed by the wind."

— James 1:6

The feelings in your heart must match the prayer requests of your mouth. When your thinking, speaking, and feelings are all in alignment, God will shower you with abounding joy. Every desire can be held in hand, every goal can be achieved, and every dream can come true. Doubt is one of the great self-saboteurs the evil one uses against you. When you begin to witness yourself thinking negatively, immediately whisper, *"Help me, God."* When you invite God into your mind, you interrupt the negative influence that had infiltrated your thinking. Once the pattern is interrupted, repeat this promise, *"I can do all things in Christ, who strengthens me."*[118]

AUGUST 10

"And I will do whatever you ask in my name,
so that the Father may be glorified in the Son."

— John 14:13

In creating the Universe, God established Law. When you understand God's perfect Law, and abide by it, you become a co-creator in His Universe. One very important Law to understand is the Law of Polarity. Simply put, for everything you experience as negative, there is an equal and opposite positive. This contrast between opposites may not always be immediately apparent. Therefore, in moments of uncertainty or hesitancy, ask God to reveal the golden opportunity, the blessing and the "silver lining" behind every dark cloud. Once you ask, prepare yourself to receive. This is often where you become stagnant. Instead of continuing to focus on the negative, have faith in God's Law, and praise Him for the positive, which is surely making its way to you.

AUGUST 11

"But to you who are listening I say: Love your enemies, do good to those who hate you, bless those who curse you, pray for those who mistreat you."

— Luke 6:27-28

One of the great lessons Jesus Christ taught was to *love your enemies*. However, what do you do when the enemy you face is your own negative thinking? Hidden in the rich metaphor of the Gospel of Luke is the secret to this enduring question: You must discipline your mind to think of love, forgiveness, and encouragement. In the same manner that a wise carpenter uses a good nail to drive out a bad nail, you can use a positive thought to replace a negative thought. Do not wrestle with the enemies of discouragement, anxiety, fear, uncertainty, and despair. Instead, call upon the name of God, and elicit the great allies of hope, encouragement, faith, and love.

AUGUST 12

"You do not have because you do not ask God."

— James 4:2

In prayer, you must be mindful to ask God for what you want, as opposed to what you currently have. Understanding the subtle difference between wanting and having elevates the power of your prayer requests, and ultimately changes the way you communicate with God, with yourself, and with the world. When you are experiencing some form of trouble, it is easy to become mentally absorbed in a pattern of thinking that only perpetuates the trouble. Even your prayers, when facing trouble, tend to energize the trouble. Therefore, obey God's Law of Polarity, and call upon your willpower to ask Him for the positive outcome you desire. God will always grant the requests of your heart, or something even greater. Ask God for what you want, and praise Him for what you will receive.

AUGUST 13

"Do not let your hearts be troubled.
Trust in God; trust also in me."

— John 14:1

When you become still in the presence of God, invite Him to renew your mind, body, and spirit. The troubles of yesterday are forgiven, and a bright future awaits you. If you remain focused on the challenges of yesterday, you remain trapped in the energy of the challenge that troubled you. However, by opening your mind to the hope and mercy of God, you allow space within this day for His love to transcend any barriers you might face. Begin each day anew, seeking the Kingdom of God that is alive within you. God is desirous to *hold you by your right hand, and lead you along paths of righteousness.*[119]

AUGUST 14

"Can a mother forget the baby at her breast and have no compassion on the child she has borne? Though she may forget, I will not forget you! See, I have engraved you on the palms of my hands."

— Isaiah 49:15-16

God has enduring faith in you. God is asking you to have enduring faith in Him. Understanding God's promise in theory and applying God's promise in your life are two different things. To demonstrate faith in God, your words must honor His promise. For example, if you proclaim faith in God's ability to supply your need, yet complain about how hard times are, your words are not in alignment and do not honor His promise. Faith in God requires your ability to turn your attention inward. If you rely on your eyes to justify your faith, you will always come up short. God knows your greatest need is a relationship with Him. The good news is that God is always present, both within you and standing alongside you.

AUGUST 15

"No one will be able to stand up against you all the days of your life. As I was with Moses, so I will be with you."

— Joshua 1:5

Moses stood on the shore of the Red Sea, and commanded the waters to part. Thousands of his followers nervously awaited, an enemy force bearing down on them, their survival dependent on Moses. With staff raised overhead, Moses said,

"Part, you seas!"

The seas did not part. Moses then walked into the sea up to his ankles, and again commanded the waters to part. Again, nothing happened. Moses continued into the waters, up to his knees, then his waist, and then his shoulders. Each time, Moses commanded the waters to part, and each time, the waters defied his command.

Finally, Moses was up to his neck in the waters. With head tilted back and staff raised overhead, Moses retained faith in God, and once again commanded the seas to part.

The seas parted, and God's promise was fulfilled.[120]

AUGUST 16

*"This is the confidence we have in
approaching God: that if we ask anything
according to His will, He hears us."*

— 1 John 5:14

God is within you. These four words have the power to radically alter the direction of your entire life. Consider the impact even a one-degree directional change could have on an airplane departing New York with the intention of landing in San Diego. A one-degree change in flight path would potentially land the plane in San Francisco, nearly four hundred miles away. When you allow God to change the direction of your life, *goodness will surely follow you all the days of your life.*[121] God's direction in your life is always for your good. The only constraint He will place is limiting how far you can fall backward. In this sense, God is your safety net and lifeline. On the other hand, the direction God can propel you forward is infinitely blessed, and entirely based on your faithfulness and courage.

AUGUST 17

"And what does the LORD require of you? To act justly, and to love mercy and to walk humbly with your God."

— Micah 6:8

Time is an ingredient in your life that you must stop trying to control. The universe was created with time as a central component of your daily experience. Time was not meant to work in opposition to you. On the contrary, time was meant to enhance the quality of your life. However, you tend to struggle against time, either trying to change the conditions of the past, or control the future events of tomorrow. Whatever intention you might have to influence or change time, any attempts are completely out of your control. This does not mean that you surrender to the past or future. On the contrary, it means you learn to live more fully today. Only in this moment, in this breath, and in this body can you experience the presence of God. Awaken to the potential this day holds for you.

AUGUST 18

"We live by faith, not by sight."
— 2 Corinthians 5:7

The physical world is a direct reflection of your inner world. By the Law of Attraction, the images you hold within your mind become the very same images you behold with your eyes. The process of attraction then folds backward on itself; what you behold with your eyes is internalized and repeated back within the visions of your mind. This interplay between projection and internalization continues for a lifetime, oftentimes completely beneath your conscious awareness. If you want to experience a new scene in your physical experience, you must first change the internalized messages you are projecting into the world. This change takes place in your mind, and in your heart. *Put your faith in the light while you have it, so that you may become a child of the light.*[122]

AUGUST 19

"Walk in all the ways that the LORD your God has commanded you, so that you may live and prosper and prolong your days in the land that you will possess."

— Deuteronomy 5:33

Deep within your soul are Godly principles that you must align your life with. One of these universal principles is loving-kindness. Over and over again in the Bible, God reminds His children to honor the power of love. You have experienced the joy that comes from giving your love to another person. Similarly, you have experienced the joy of being loved. However, the greatest source of love is the love you give to yourself, and to God. To love God means to love yourself, and by loving yourself, you love God. Self-love is reflected in the quality of your thinking, speaking, and actions. Loving God is reflected by stillness in His presence, and an open heart to His embrace.

AUGUST 20

*"I will walk among you and be your
God, and you will be my people."*

— Leviticus 26:12

Health professionals agree that people who want to become physically fit should consider a daily program of walking. Sustained walking over a lifetime will improve fitness, health, muscle-tone, and will strengthen your heart. God wants you to know that a lifetime of walking with Him will also have many health benefits. When you walk with God, you experience courage, peacefulness, assuredness, and faith. To walk with God means you must abide by His Word and His Law. The physical act of walking benefits you in the world, while spiritual walking benefits you in the Kingdom of God. Spiritual walking is accomplished in stillness and silence. By spending time each day simply being still in the presence of God, you rejuvenate, restore, and replenish both the outer body, and the inner body. Think how great a tree a small acorn grows. This is the same greatness that is alive within you. Nourish the seeds of potential that God has planted in your soul.

AUGUST 21

"Do not let your hearts be troubled. Trust in God."

— John 14:1

You have a tendency to struggle to work things out before their time has come. This is like planting a garden in the morning, and then digging up the seeds in the evening to see if there has been any growth. You will experience a blessed peacefulness when you accept the boundaries and limitations of living one day at a time. When something comes to your attention that troubles you, become still and ask God whether it is something you can do anything about today. God will help you focus on what can be accomplished and resolved today. Leave tomorrow in the capable hands of God. When you live close to God, your life becomes pure, simple, and uncluttered. You will know you are in God's presence when things that used to trouble you lose their power, and instead *become recognized as light and momentary afflictions securing your eternal glory.*[123]

AUGUST 22

*"Jesus told his disciples, 'I have told you
these things, so that in me you may have peace.
In this world you will have trouble. But take
heart! I have overcome the world.'"*

— John 16:33

Do not let anything disturb the great peace residing within you. The more challenging the set of circumstances you face, the more strength God will provide you. God will always supply everything you need, at the exact time and place that you need it most. However, He will not provide to you today the needs you have for tomorrow. This understanding can form the basis for an unshakeable confidence and courage. God knows what challenges you will face each day, and He is eager to equip you for the great adventures this day has in store for you. Your job is to turn to God for strength, and *not rely on your own understanding or capacity*.[124] Every circumstance and situation in your life will perfectly match your ability to be victorious over it.

AUGUST 23

*"We who have fled to take hold of the hope offered
to us may be greatly encouraged. We have this hope
as an anchor for the soul, firm and secure."*

— Hebrews 6:18-19

God is conditioning you to remain close to Him and to *anchor your life into His presence.* Every moment of your life is an opportunity for you to witness the presence of God. God is desirous of your attention, and He wants you to remain focused on Him. At all times and under every condition, God wants to be the anchor of your soul. Ultimately, you will mature to the realization that nothing is good or bad, positive or negative, but your thinking makes it so. When you grasp the reality that everything you attract into your life is for your benefit, then you will begin to understand the magnificent love God has for you. You only feel hopeless to the extent your anchor becomes loose. Cling tightly to God, and He will cling tightly to you.

AUGUST 24

"My soul finds rest in God alone; my salvation comes from Him. He alone is my rock and my salvation; He is my fortress."

— Psalm 62:1-2

At the center of every castle was the fortified tower. A last line of defense, the fortified tower was designed to protect the city inhabitants from an attack. In the event the castle walls were breached, an alarm would sound, and city residents would run to the safety of the tower. Once inside the tower, their safety was secured. God is your fortified tower. When you feel the world has attacked the boundaries of your physical and mental limitations, turn to God. Withdraw into His presence, and He will be your salvation, your strength, and your fortified fortress.

AUGUST 25

*"For I am the LORD your God, who takes
hold of your right hand and says to you,
'Do not fear; I will help you.'"*
— Isaiah 41:13

There is an open and golden road ahead of you. To walk by faith means to trust that despite what today might have in store, your future is secure. Along the path of life, Jesus Christ is your traveling companion, and he is eager to help you navigate the twists, turns, peaks, and valleys of your journey. Your responsibility is to stop focusing on the mistakes of the past, and to cease worrying about what lies ahead. Trust in God, and believe the way before you is safe and secure, in spite of how it might currently look. This is the faith-walk God calls for you to undertake upon the great adventure of your life.

AUGUST 26

"Cast your cares on the LORD, and He will sustain you; He will never let the righteous fall."

— Psalm 55:22

Trust that God is big enough, strong enough, and willing enough to sustain you each day of your life. When you feel overwhelmed, instead of continuing to struggle and expend your energy, give your concerns to God. Giving concerns to God helps you gain perspective over what you can influence, and what is best left in the hands of God. When you gain clarity over what you can and cannot influence, you will increase your effect and potential for success. A small percentage of your focused energy, when directed on the right parts of your life, will have a rate of return that will astonish you. In the world, you were taught more work is equal to more return. However, God wants you to realize the error in this thinking. It is never a matter of the quantity of your effort, but rather the quality.

AUGUST 27

"Blessed is the man who trusts in the LORD, whose confidence is in Him. He will be like a tree planted by the water that sends out its roots by the stream."

— Jeremiah 17:7-8

God created nature to help you learn certain principles of spiritual living. The root system and base of a tree are extremely strong and resilient. In a storm, the branches may blow back and forth and even bend against the wind. However, if you look closely, the base of the tree is motionless, and the roots are completely unaffected. During your life, you can benefit from taking on the qualities of a great tree. As the storms of life come, do not resist their force. Be flexible and accommodating, and do not feel overwhelmed. Your security is in your base and root system, which is grounded in the strength of God.

AUGUST 28

"I will refresh the weary and satisfy the faint."
— Jeremiah 31:25

As a child of God, you were born with divine creative power. You and the source of creation are one and the same. You are a co-creator with God; your birthright is one of infinite and expansive manifesting potential. As Jesus Christ taught his disciples, you are a gardener, toiling in the fertile soil of your mind. The seeds of your mind, when correctly planted, will grow into your heart's desire. What you focus your attention on will increase in your life. When you ask for health, you are given health. When you seek love, you will find love. When you knock upon the door of abundance, God will overflow your cup.

AUGUST 29

"Before they call I will answer; while
they are still speaking I will hear."

— Isaiah 65:24

In any given moment of your life, you can witness the quality of your thinking, the quality of your breathing, and the quality of your physical posture. This ability to witness creates a small space, or gap, between your witnessing self, and your thinking, breathing, and physicality. In this space lies the peace of God. Learn to cultivate this space in the early morning hours as you become silent and still in the presence of God. Over time and with practice, you will notice the gap between thoughts begin to expand. God's gentle caress will wash over you like a cool mist, covering you with His peace. As you journey through the adventures of your day, this shield-like covering will protect your mind, allowing you to continually experience His grace and mercy. *Blessed and happy is the one who takes refuge in the peace of God.*[125]

AUGUST 30

"Jesus replied, 'Apart from me, you can do nothing.'"
— John 15:5

When you feel overwhelmed and weighed down by your troubles, remember that God is eager to help carry your burdens. Instead of giving your attention to the troubles, give your attention to the power of God. There is immense strength available when you break away from the world and allow your mind to be restored by the peace of God's presence. When you view your problems from the elevated perspective of God's grace and mercy, they will seem *light and temporary*. Even in adverse circumstances, you can find joy in the One who overcame the world.

AUGUST 31

*"You have been my hope, O Sovereign
LORD, my confidence since my youth."*

— Psalm 71:5

There is a tremendous difference between your life experiences, and your thoughts about the experiences. Your thoughts about everything you perceive determine your perception and reaction, and shape your reality. In fact, your life is ultimately the manifestation of your individual thoughts. God wants to express His love, creativity, and intelligence through your thinking. However, the anxiety and worry caused by your automatic reaction to your perceptions blocks God's full expression of love to flow through you. When you become still in God's presence and calm the wave impulses of your habitual thinking, God is able to fill your mind with His light. The more time you spend in His light, the more light you reflect through your life.

SEPTEMBER

---

*"Cease striving and know that I am God;
I will be exalted among the nations, I
will be exalted in the earth."*

— Psalm 46:10

SEPTEMBER 1

"Put your hope in the LORD, for the LORD is unfailing love and with Him is full redemption."

— Psalm 130:7

When you trust God, you are able to find refuge in His protective embrace. Sometimes, trusting God requires the conscious use of your willpower. As you journey through the adventures of this day, you may encounter things that make you anxious, including your own thinking. When you are not aware of the rise of negative thoughts, they can easily consume you, and influence your words and actions. Therefore, as Jesus Christ taught his disciples, *"Be on alert at all times."*[126] You must use your willpower and remain vigilant in order to "catch" the negative worry-thoughts before they take hold of you. Rather than being consumed by your thinking, pay attention to the space between your thoughts. Even a sliver of space allows your higher self the necessary time for God's grace to weed out worry, anxiety, and distress. *In the shadow of God's wings, take refuge until the calamities have passed by.*[127]

SEPTEMBER 2

*"Blessed is the man who trusts in the
LORD, whose confidence is in Him."*

— Jeremiah 17:7

God wants to lead you through this day. Have the courage to follow God, and trust that His leadership will direct you along glorious paths, and protect you from pitfalls along the way. Your mission is to stay alert to the mighty presence of God, and keep your eyes fixed on Him. Instead of worrying what today holds, or what tasks must be completed, focus on drawing close to God. Discipline yourself to press into God, trusting that everything before you will be for your good. God is with you. God is for you. *God is fighting your battles for you.*[128]

SEPTEMBER 3

"When you pass through the waters, I will be with you; and when you pass through the rivers, they will not sweep you over."

— Isaiah 43:2

A young boy stood on the shore next to a fast-moving river, eager to cross to the other side. However, the rush of the water and his inability to see a clear path across the river made him hesitate to take the necessary first step. For several hours, the boy searched and looked for a path across the dangerous waters. Suddenly, the boy noticed what appeared to be a rock shimmering just above the water's surface. The rock seemed to beckon the boy to take a step, and begin his journey across the water. With great faith, the young boy timidly stepped off the shore, onto the rock. From the new vantage point of the rock within the water, the boy noticed another rock in front of him, which had not been visible from the shore. As soon as he stepped onto this rock, another appeared before him. And so it was the young boy safely crossed the river to the far shore.

SEPTEMBER 4

*"If I rise on the wings of the dawn, if I settle
on the far side of the sea, even there your hand
will guide me, your hand will hold me fast."*

— Psalm 139:10

You were hard-wired from birth to search for a resting place. You long to find peace in the world around you, in your circumstances, and in your immediate environment. However, you must realize the external world is in constant flux. As long as you search for stillness in a fluctuating world, you will be met with disappointment. The good news is that stillness and peace are always available. The moment you turn your attention away from the external world, and focus on the internal universe inside you, God's Kingdom will open before you. The awareness of God's Kingdom will be felt with the heart, not seen with the eyes. *For behold, the Kingdom of God is within you!*[129]

SEPTEMBER 5

"We are the temple of the living God. As God has said, 'I will live with them and walk among them, and I will be their God, and they will be My people.'"

— 2 Corinthians 6:16

You must learn set aside time each day to be holy in God's presence. The word "holy" means: *"To be set aside for sacred use."* Therefore, when you become still in the presence of God, you allow the sacredness and divinity of your mind to become one with His omnipresence. In other words, you become both "holy" and "whole" in God's presence. When you set aside time to be with God, He will begin to transform your mind, body and heart. You will experience God's *holiness and wholeness.* You will be renewed, lifted up, and restored. *You will be lifted up on the wings of an eagle.* In the same manner you are able to absorb the healing benefits of sunshine, your soul soaks in the glorious Light of God, which then radiates through you into the world.[130]

SEPTEMBER 6

"Be very careful to keep the commandment and the Law that Moses the servant of the LORD gave to you: to love the LORD your God, to walk in all His ways, to obey His commands, to hold fast to Him and to serve Him with all your heart and all your soul."

— Joshua 22:5

You tend to regard things that you can perceive with your senses as real. Things that are not readily available to your senses you generally think of as unreal or imaginary. God desperately wants you to realize that *your thoughts and words are real*. More than simply real, there is a mighty power in your thoughts and words. Creative energy resonates throughout God's Universe every time you speak. Every word you speak is like a seed, which holds the ability to produce an effect in your life. Therefore, guard your tongue, disciplining yourself to honor the great teaching of Jesus Christ that *your speaking influences the quality of your life.*[131] Ensure the seeds you plant are rich in light, love, kindness, abundance, health, and positivity.

SEPTEMBER 7

*"God guides the humble in what is
right and teaches them His way."*
— Psalm 25:9

Both conscious and subconscious thoughts have an effect on your life experience. A thought held and repeated enough times in your mind will seep into the universal consciousness and begin to produce like effects in your life. At any given moment, you can take an assessment of your habitual and perhaps even unconscious thinking by reflecting on the conditions of your daily life experiences. If you are facing trouble of a persistent type, it may be that a thought planted long ago is finally beginning to produce in your reality. The greatest self-empowering step you can take is to fully accept responsibility for the conditions in your life. The empowerment comes not from faulting yourself, but from loving yourself and acknowledging the great power your mind contains. Then, in the stillness and peaceful presence of God, invite Him to elevate the quality of your thinking.

SEPTEMBER 8

*"The LORD is good to those whose hope
is in Him, to the one who seeks Him."*

— Lamentations 3:25

It is important for you to understand the correlation between thoughts and feelings. For example, when you begin to witness yourself experiencing feelings of worry or fear, you must discipline your mind to focus on thoughts of trust and thankfulness instead. The interplay between your thinking and feeling, and feeling and thinking, is immense. To simplify the process, you must focus both your thoughts and feelings on God. The choice to focus on God is a choice you may need to make hundreds of times a day. However, do not despair, for each time you turn from fear to love, your will-power is strengthened, and the bond between you and God will grow stronger. Thought patterns of love repeated numerous times will become etched into your mind, and the pathway between you and God will take on the quality of a super-highway, speeding you to His welcoming embrace.

SEPTEMBER 9

"Blessed is he whose hope is in God."

— Psalm 146:5

Everything you desire in this moment exists as formless energy in God's Universe. What your mind can conceive, you have the divine right to receive. Therefore, the only thing preventing you from obtaining the desires of your heart is your own limited thinking. In order to become a co-creator with God, and receive the countless blessings He has stored up for you, do the following:

1. *Seek first the Kingdom of God.*[132]

2. Focus on what you desire, not the lack of it.

3. Praise God for His ability *to provide all your needs.*

When your thoughts, words, emotions, and actions are in harmony with God, the desires of your heart will be effortlessly placed at your feet. *Seek first God's Kingdom, and his righteousness, and everything else will be given to you.*[133]

SEPTEMBER 10

"Jesus taught his disciples saying, 'If you believe,
you will receive whatever you ask for in prayer.'"
— Matthew 21:22

God created you to experience the fulfillment of your dreams and goals. God is your champion, and He wants to help in the accomplishment of your vision for an ideal life. When you are in perfect alignment with God, inspiration, divine guidance, and creativity will become a natural state of being for you. Discipline yourself to hold the images of your heart's desire in your mind's eye. The power of your mind to attract the images it holds in place is immense. Great athletes use visualization to help prepare them for exceptional physical performances. In the same fashion, you can visualize your ideal conditions across the screen of your mind, trusting they will take form in your life. Remember that God wants to be an active participant in the creation of your life. Together, you and God are like foreman and architect, working together to construct the life of your dreams.

SEPTEMBER 11

*"No eye has seen, no ear has heard,
no mind has conceived what God has
prepared for those who love Him."*

— 1 Corinthians 2:9

In order to attract good conditions into your life, you must hold good thoughts in your mind. Your mind has immense magnetic pulling-power, and over time, everything that is within the magnetic force field of your mind will become your reality. You must remember the attracting power of your mind does not have an ability to discern the quality of what it attracts. The pulling-power of your mind will simply draw towards itself anything it focuses upon. Therefore, you must continually refocus your mind upon *what is good, kind, righteous, just, and loving.*[134] The fastest way to change the conditions of your life is to focus your mind upon God. When God becomes the sole center-point of your thinking, *goodness and love will surely accompany you all the days of your life.*[135]

SEPTEMBER 12

*"God is able to make all grace abound to you,
so that in all things at all times, having all that
you need, you will abound in every good work."*
— 2 Corinthians 9:8

Fix your eyes on Jesus Christ, for he is the same yesterday, today and forever more.[136] You have a tendency to focus your attention upon the matters of the world. Like an ocean during a storm, the matters of the world are constantly tossing about, changing direction, and existing in a perpetually unsteady state. Therefore, you must discipline yourself to discern the difference between what is changing, and *the one who always remains the same.* Consider a sailor lost at sea who searches for the welcoming beacon of the lighthouse or the navigational certainty of the North Star. Because God's presence is always the same, He is the perfect focal point for your mind and navigational compass for your life. Although a *still small voice*, God's presence is within you at all times, and under all circumstances. There is nothing you can do, and no place you can go, that would distance you from God's love.

SEPTEMBER 13

"God tends His flock like a shepherd: He gathers the lambs in His arms and carries them close to His heart."

— Isaiah 40:11

You can learn to live from a place of security in God. When you view life from the perspective that God is the shepherd of your soul, you will begin to handle problems with a light touch. When you realize you have wandered out from the security of His watchfulness, simply stop moving and become still. One of the lessons taught in wilderness survival is that when you recognize you are lost, stop walking and assess your conditions and surroundings. Although counterintuitive, continuing to walk aimlessly through a forest only decreases the prospect of help finding you. Like a lost lamb that becomes still and cries out for help, sometimes your greatest strength is your ability to become still, and call upon the name of God. When you call out to God for help, He will find you and gather you into His loving arms.

SEPTEMBER 14

"God will command His angels concerning you to guard you in all your ways; they will lift you up in their hands, so that you will not strike your foot against a stone."

— Psalm 91:11

God is able to do more than you could ever ask or imagine. Even your wildest dreams and goals pale in comparison to God's ability to bless your life. Therefore, your challenge is to experience life through the perspective of God, rather than your own limited understanding. Remember that God is continually at work in your life. He is both within you, hovering over you, and on the path slightly ahead of you. God is simultaneously helping you today, while preparing the way for you tomorrow. Although you are taking in life one experience at a time, God has your big picture in mind, and is continually bringing you one step closer to your prayers and desires. The great secret to receiving your heartfelt prayers is to continually thank God for their receipt, trusting that in His perfect time, *you will receive immeasurably more than you can ask for or imagine.*[137]

SEPTEMBER 15

"'My grace is sufficient for you, for my power is made perfect in weakness,' says the LORD."

— 2 Corinthians 12:9

God's thoughts are greater than your thoughts, and God's ways are greater than your ways.[138] This truth can liberate you, and open you to receive the riches God has in store for you. Although God is vastly higher than you, He is also within you. Therefore, do not allow worry to consume your mind. Trust that God has your best interests in the palm of His hand. Leave the outcomes up to God and have the courage to follow wherever He may lead you. Concentrate on taking just one step at a time with God, enjoying the ebb and flow of His direction. When you are in a pasture, take time to rest in His rejuvenating presence. When you stand before a mountain, hold tightly to His hand. Enjoy the rhythm of your life, and embrace God who is your constant companion at all times.

SEPTEMBER 16

"I command you today to love the LORD your God, to walk in His ways, and to keep His commandments, decrees and Laws; then you will live and increase, and the LORD your God will bless you."

— Deuteronomy 30:16

It takes immense willpower to become still in the presence of God. The challenge only increases when the world is clamoring for your attention. However, you must remember that nothing is more important than spending quality time with God. When you become still and allow God to renew your mind and body, you are richly blessed. If you dismiss this time with God, your habitual ways of behaving and conditioned ways of thinking will lead you astray. Furthermore, remember to always rejoice more in the giver of gifts, rather than the gift itself. Anything can become your focal point, including possessions, worldly relationships, and even your own thinking. When God is the ultimate desire of your mind and heart, you are safe from the illusion of self-sufficiency and worldly satisfactions.

SEPTEMBER 17

"If you do whatever I command you and walk in my ways and do what is right in my eyes by keeping my statutes and commands, then I will be with you."

— 1 Kings 3:14

The Word of God is alive with power, opportunity, and strength. Bible verse repeated both out loud and in the silence of your mind will heal your heart, and restore your weary soul. The more often you repeat God's Word, the greater His Word in your life will be. Like any skill, repetition is the first law of learning. When you have repeated God's Word so often that His voice plays like background music in your mind, then you will have made progress. Grace will become your natural state of being, and you will increasingly grow in the likeness of His son, Jesus Christ.

SEPTEMBER 18

"Blessed are they who keep His statues and seek Him with all their heart. They do nothing wrong; they walk in His ways."

— Psalm 119:1-3

A heart like Christ requires a daily commitment to abiding in faith and righteous thinking. You must learn to think constructively and positively of all persons, all things, all events, and all circumstances. In addition, and perhaps most importantly, you must discipline yourself to think positively of yourself. By appraising yourself, others and circumstances from a Christ-like point of view, your conditions will change as a direct result of your thinking. As you discipline yourself to look for the good, you will begin to move towards the good, and attract more of that which is good into your life. From a Christ-like perspective, your mind will be lifted to heavenly realms where joy, peace, and tranquility will accompany you all the days of your life.

SEPTEMBER 19

"I am the LORD your God, who teaches you what is best for you, who directs you in the way you should go."

— Isaiah 48:17

God has carefully choreographed everything you have experienced in life up to this very moment. Because God knows what is best for you, everything you have experienced in life has been for your good. Through God's perfect plan and divine timing, your life is unfolding according to His glory. You are safe, you are protected, and you are in the hands of God. Rejoice in the certainty that God has great plans, opportunities, appointments, prosperity, love, adventure, and service in store for you. Remain positive in your mind, holding strong to the anchor of God's promise.

SEPTEMBER 20

"Blessed is the man who does not walk in the counsel of the wicked or stand in the way of sinners or sit in the seat of mockers."

— Psalm 1: 1-2

God is speaking to you from the depths of your soul. Sometimes, because God's voice quietly resides within you, it takes time for His assurances to reach up from your soul into your consciousness. Therefore, you must learn to discern the difference between God's voice of love, and the evil one's voice of accusation and doubt. God speaks to you in love tones, lifting you up and rejoicing over you. Pay attention to the feelings of expansiveness and openness, for these are signs you have drawn close to God. Also, discipline yourself to pause before responding to people or situations, giving God an opportunity to speak and act through you. Weed out from the garden of your mind all doubt, negativity, and fear. Because God is within you, His presence can rise up through you, and take permanent residence in your mind.

SEPTEMBER 21

"'I will make an everlasting covenant with them: I will never stop doing good to them,' says the LORD."
— Jeremiah 32:40

The challenge set out before you is to learn to live above your circumstances. This is accomplished by following the example of Jesus Christ: *keep your eyes focused on God and not the world.* Trouble and distress are a natural part of the fabric of the universe. However, they were never meant to consume you or distract you from God. Consider this example: Does the sky complain about the conditions of the weather that pass below it? Certainly not! The sky simply holds space for the passing weather, without judgment, attachment, or aversion. In the same fashion, you can learn to live above any condition that passes before the screen of your eyes and mind. Learning to live above your circumstances helps you gain perspective on life, and enables you to focus on what is important and what is not.

SEPTEMBER 22

"For God so loved the world that He gave His one and only Son, that whoever believes in him shall not perish but have eternal life."

— John 3:16

Where your awareness goes, your energy will flow. To develop a heart like Christ, you must continually realign your awareness to the presence of God. Develop the discipline to take a break from the demands of the day to spend time with God. As you draw close to God, bring awareness to the quality of your breathing. Is it fast and anxious, or slow and steady? Your breath is the bridge between your mind, body, and spirit. The act of taking a deep breath in, and a slow breath out, will help to calm the turbulence of your mind. God will reveal Himself to you by feelings of comfort, peacefulness, and tranquility. When you feel distant from God, it was not God who moved. God is always with you. God is always for you. *God is always fighting your battles for you.*[139] His holy presence is only one breath away.

SEPTEMBER 23

"Agree with God, and be at peace;
thereby good will come to you."

— John 22:21

God wants to be part of every aspect of your life. Bring all conceivable details before Him, and resist the temptation to do things on your own. Ask God to help you discern where to focus your energy and life force. You have a special purpose to fulfill, and in order to succeed, you must ensure wise and disciplined use of time. The best use of your time is always time spent alone with God. Even though your rational mind will attempt to convince you that you are not doing anything, nothing could be further from the truth. When you spend time with God, He is able to invest the time in your favor, and to multiply the return on your behalf. Spiritual time outweighs worldly time one hundred to one.

SEPTEMBER 24

*"My flesh and my heart may fail, but God is
the strength of my heart and my portion forever."*
— Psalm 73:26

The feelings and emotions you entertain will attract circumstances, events, people, and ultimately an entire reality that will perfectly match your energetic set point. This is why Jesus Christ taught that whatever you *feel in your heart you will become your reality.*[140] One of the best ways to establish a feeling of peacefulness, love, contentment, and abundance is to spend time alone with God. Because God is complete, whole and absolute, when you spend time with Him, these qualities begin to take shape in your life. Turn your attention inward, close your eyes, and become still. Gradually, the turmoil of your mind will calm, and God's love will envelop you. *Seek first the Kingdom of God, and everything else will fall perfectly into place.*[141]

SEPTEMBER 25

"Do not be anxious about anything, but in everything by prayer and petition with thanksgiving let your requests be made known to God."

— Philippians 4:6

You have a tendency to accomplish things through your own effort. By sheer stubbornness and the expense of great energy, you manage to set and achieve worldly goals. This method will ultimately deplete you and exhaust your life force. Thankfully, there is another way. The moments you are in harmony with God and abide in His holy presence, you instantly become available to the blessings He has stored up for you. Everything is prepared for you, countless riches eagerly await your receipt, and goodness accounts for all the days of your life. Let go. Let God.

SEPTEMBER 26

*"Do not conform yourselves to the standards
of this world, but let God transform you inwardly
by a complete change of your mind. Then you will
be able to know the will of God—what is good
and is pleasing to Him and is perfect."*

— Romans 12:2

Jesus Christ taught the faith of a child could access all the riches of God's Kingdom. Through the innocence and simplicity of childlike understanding, all the glory of God's Kingdom would be available. The question then becomes: *"What can you learn from a child?"* A child abides by God's Law of *"Ask and you shall receive."* A child knows the limitations of their ability to self-provide. When a desire arises outside the child's ability to accomplish or fulfill, they ask their mother or father to provide for them. A child asks with faith and positive expectancy that their desire (or something greater) will be fulfilled. A child asks for *what* they desire, not *how* their desire will be supplied. A heart like Christ means an ability to embrace the spirit of a child, and bring before the throne of God all your needs. You will have, when you ask.

SEPTEMBER 27

*"Even though I walk through the darkest valley,
I will fear no evil, for you are with me; your rod
and your staff, they comfort me."*
— Psalm 23:4

To obey the Word of God necessitates comprehension and compliance with God's Laws. A life lived in accordance with God's Law results in harmony, peacefulness, and spiritual fulfillment. One critical Law for you to understand is the Law of Sacrifice. The Law of Sacrifice means your ability to exchange something of lesser value for something of greater value. To obey this Law is to bountifully receive your rightful measure of health, prosperity, success, fulfillment, and happiness. When you sacrifice your time to be still and silent in God's presence, you are following the Law of Sacrifice. By giving up your time for God, you receive His blessing, and the restoration of your mind and body. Time spent with God is more important than time spent in any worldly endeavor. Furthermore, with practice, you will develop the ability to remain aware of God's presence even in the accomplishment of your worldly duties.

SEPTEMBER 28

*"In all thy ways acknowledge Him,
and He shall direct thy paths."*

— Proverbs 3:6

You must come to respect the truth that your thinking will influence the way you see your environment. In other words, when you change the way you think about something, what you think about will begin to change. Your ability to consciously choose your thoughts in response to your environment is a marvelous gift from God. The gift of independent thinking can liberate you and set you free. The first step in gaining control of your thinking is to witness your own thoughts. Then, gently begin to align your thoughts with the Word of God. Your ability to hear the Word of God will increase when your thinking shifts from the world to His presence. God is available to you every moment of your life. He longs to make contact with you, but you cannot reach Him in the past or future. Discipline yourself to continually realign your awareness to the present moment, which is where the presence of God resides.

SEPTEMBER 29

"Therefore, since we are surrounded by such a great cloud of witnesses, let us throw off everything that hinders and the sin that so easily entangles. And let us run with perseverance the race marked out for us."

— Hebrews 12:1

You must develop the qualities of a brave centurion guard, protecting the fortress of your mind from the invading enemies of negativity and despair. When you are weary or fatigued, the forces of self-pity are the greatest threat to your peace of mind and awareness of God's presence. Do not tempt the negative downward gravitational pull of self-pity, and stay far away from the frail edges of its dark pit. It is far easier for you to remain away from the edge than to climb back up out of the pit. The best way to remain on guard against self-pity is to continually look for the positive in every situation, and to occupy your mind with gratefulness and praise of God. The more time you spend in the light of God's presence, the stronger your faith will become, and greater endurance you will have to *run the race that is set before you.*

SEPTEMBER 30

"Yet to all who did receive him, to those who believed in his name, he gave the right to become children of God."

— John 1:12

When you allow God to lead you through the great adventure of life, the journey becomes much more enjoyable. You are able to see people and situations through the peacefulness that only His presence can provide. You will happily discover the more trust you place in God, the higher the perspective you will gain over the world. God will lift your eyes and heart, providing you with understanding, compassion, and serenity. When you completely entrust your life to God, a gentle strength will radiate both within and around you.

OCTOBER

"As for me, I watch in hope for the LORD, I wait for God my Savior; my God will hear me."

— Micah 7:7

OCTOBER 1

"Do not be afraid. Stand firm and you will see the deliverance the LORD will bring to you today."

— Exodus 14:13

Because your mind is so intimately entangled with your physical body and all of its worldly necessities, your soul sometimes loses touch with the omnipresence of God. Therefore, you must discipline yourself to remember that God, the supreme creator of the Universe, whose very image you were made in, is always present within you. God's creative and manifesting power is hidden within you, just as the presence and power of a tree is hidden within a small seed. The small seed planted in proper soil will bring forth a great tree. Similarly, when you spend time in the presence of God, His divine nature will manifest itself greatly in your life.

OCTOBER 2

"The LORD longs to be gracious to you;
He rises to show you His compassion."

— Isaiah 30:18

When your conscious awareness is focused exclusively on the world, you become easily preoccupied with physical wants and needs. Your mind acts like a vice and is constrained by the limitations of your physical body. Because you are only focused on the body and the material needs it demands, you tend to think of yourself as contained by the body, and you lose sight of your spiritual self. When your senses focus on the limits of your body and the world, your thinking becomes equally limited. However, when you turn your attention inward and meditate on God, you allow for His presence to expand within you. You, your meditation, and the focus of your meditation merge into one. When your mind focuses on the unlimited nature of God, your mind expands to the infinite creative potential of His Universe, which is both within and all around you.

OCTOBER 3

*"The eternal God is your refuge, and
underneath are His everlasting arms."*
— Deuteronomy 33:27

Keep your eyes and heart focused on God. When waves of adversity and trouble wash over you, it is easy to become swept out into a sea of negativity. When caught in a rip tide, attempting to swim against the current is a futile waste of energy. Similarly, as your circumstances consume more and more of your attention, you must discipline yourself to hold tightly to the hand of God. His presence is with you always, and He will never allow you to face a challenge greater than your ability to overcome. One of the greatest dangers you face is the temptation of worrying about tomorrow, and attempting to carry the burdens of the future with you today. Open your eyes and your heart to the presence of God who is with you now. Remain present to the presence of God, *and take refuge in His everlasting arms.*

OCTOBER 4

"May we turn our hearts to Him, to walk in all His ways and to keep the commands, decrees and regulations He gave our fathers."

— 1 Kings 8:58

Discipline yourself to look continually in the direction of God. The direction of your life will gravitate towards what you are paying attention to. Therefore, by continually realigning your focus upon God, you move closer to His presence. Furthermore, because His presence is like a powerful magnet, even a brief glance in His direction can have a positive effect in your life. Whenever you need comfort, look to God for the warmth and security only He can provide. As God comforts you, you become a channel of peace for others, allowing God's embrace to flow through you into the world.

OCTOBER 5

*"Do you not know? Have you not heard? The LORD
is the everlasting God, the Creator of the ends of
the earth. He will not grow tired or weary, and His
understanding no one can fathom. He gives strength
to the weary and increases the power of the weak."*

— Isaiah 40:28-29

You must take whatever necessary steps are required to remain calm and peaceful. Your ordinary life tends to function like a pendulum, ceaselessly swinging back and forth between the extremes of happiness and sadness, contentment and unease, peace and trouble. In the center of the swing and between the extremes there is a point of stillness that is beckoning. God wants to sing love songs to you of calmness. This is what Jesus Christ meant when he promised, *"My peace will be with you."* Calmness and peacefulness is the living and loving presence of God within you.

OCTOBER 6

"May the God of peace equip you with everything good for doing His will, and may He work through you what is pleasing to Him."
— Hebrews 13:20

Whatever you desire to be, you may become now—in this very moment. Non-accomplishment, delay, and lack are a result of your perpetual postponement and idle thinking. Thoughts of self-doubt can be transformed into thoughts of confidence and intrinsic motivation. By God's Law of Polarity, you intuitively have the ability to experience the contrast between positive and negative. When you understand this Law, you shall have the ability to become today your ideal self of tomorrow. This is what Jesus Christ meant when he said, *"When you pray, whatever you pray for, believe that you already have it, and it shall be yours."*[142] Discipline yourself to listen and obey the Word of God, and the voice of your spiritual center. Nurture the seeds of faith, courage, optimism, and positive expectancy that reside in the fertile soil of your mind.

OCTOBER 7

"But the LORD stood with me and strengthened me, so that through me the proclamation might be fully accomplished, and that all the Gentiles might hear; I was rescued from the lion's mouth."

— 2 Timothy 4:17

You can demonstrate your trust and faith in God by becoming still in His presence. When you put aside the worldly obligations, tasks and to-do lists that demand your attention, and instead spend time focusing on the presence of God, you are richly blessed. This quality is known in the spiritual world as *"stillness before action."* When you embrace this practice, you will develop a keen sense of what is important and what is actually a distraction. Doing countless unnecessary activities robs you of energy and motivation for doing the things that really matter. From a point of stillness, God is able to provide you with divine guidance, *enabling you to accomplish more through Jesus Christ who strengthens you then you can accomplish on your own.*[143]

OCTOBER 8

"As soon as I pray you answer me; you encourage me by giving me strength."

— Psalm 138:3

One of the key lessons Jesus Christ taught through vivid imagery was that rain would fall on the righteous and the unrighteous. The difference, however, was that the righteous person had built their house upon a foundation of rock. When the rains came and many people were swept away, the righteous remained steadfast through the Word of God. Christ taught that the righteous honor God, love God, and call God a friend. Begin today with the agreement that God is calling you to have faith that is bold, courageous, and persistent. The mindset and self-talk for a heart like Christ is, *"I can handle it. I am ready and greater than any storm I face. Almighty God, the Creator of the Universe, is within me, strengthening me. I am equipped, empowered, anointed, and blessed with God's favor. I am strong for God is with me."* Build your life on the rock of God.

OCTOBER 9

"After you have suffered for a little while, the God of all grace, who called you to His eternal glory in Christ, will perfect, confirm, strengthen and establish you."
— 1 Peter 5:10

The light of God shines evenly throughout the world. However, because of delusive ignorance and false belief in separateness, not all of God's children receive and reflect His light alike. Sunlight falls on both a lump of coal and a diamond, but only the diamond is able to absorb and reflect the light in brilliant beauty.[144] You have within you all that is required to absorb and reflect the light of God. To become a Child of God is not something you have to do. In fact, there is nothing you can do to make God love you more than He already does. Rather, all you have to do to receive God's light and love is to become still in His presence. In stillness, God will anoint you and restore your mind. You will awaken as if from a deep sleep, and rise into your divine nature. God will elevate the quality of your thinking, and you will know the truth. You are blessed. You are magnificent. You are a child of God.

OCTOBER 10

"My hand will sustain him;
surely my arm will strengthen him."

— Psalm 89:21

It is easy to become mislead by the popular misconception that peace can be attained through more wealth, possessions, insurance, and security systems. When you reflect on the nature of your thinking, you will discover that a great deal of time and mental energy is devoted to trying to create this false sense of security. However, the peace of God is independent of any and all circumstances. When you experience God's everlasting peace, a feeling of comfort, protection, and contentment will envelop you. *Though you may lose the world, if you have the peace of God, you will be rich indeed.*[145]

OCTOBER 11

"You will make known to me the path of life;
In Your presence is fullness of joy; In Your
right hand there are pleasures forever."

— Psalm 16:11

You must learn to identify and remove the misleading habits of your mind. When you become still and begin to witness your thinking, you will notice the tendency of your mind to project itself into the future or the past. In either case, this projection of the mind leads to feelings of unrest and anxiety. Despite the temptation to mentally dwell in the past or future, remain focused on the present moment. It is only in the present that you are able to experience the presence of God. When you catch yourself in the past of future, simply return your attention to your breath, and whisper, *"God, help me."* God is always with you. He is always by your side and eager to be of comfort to you. However, you must meet Him in this moment, in this body, and in this breath. Return your attention to the present, and you will experience His presence. *Today is the day the Lord has made. Rejoice and be glad in it!*[146]

OCTOBER 12

"You will seek Me and find Me when you search for Me with all your heart."

— Jeremiah 29:13

Your ability to think and speak affords you with creative and manifesting power. Therefore, you must learn to exercise discernment of your thinking, because your speaking is a direct reflection of your thinking. In other words, you must think before you speak. In the silence of your heart, ask yourself if what you intend to say will bring peace, love, and happiness to you and others. By spending time alone with God, you will develop skillfulness in your speaking, and your words will be of great comfort to all. When you are still in the presence of God, your mind will be renewed, and your thinking will be elevated. Think of love. Think of life. Think of God.

OCTOBER 13

"Whatever you ask in my name, this I will do, that the Father may be glorified in the Son. If you ask me anything in my name, I will do it."

— John 14:13-14

The desires of your heart must be in perfect alignment with your thoughts and words. When you learn to think and speak exclusively about what you desire, God will provide everything you request. The challenge, therefore, is to continue to think and speak about what you desire, even if your current reality does not immediately reflect your intention. Develop the discipline to think and speak with only positive expectancy, optimism, and personal belief. It is far better to remain silent than to defeat yourself with negativity. Vow to trust in God's love and grand plan for your life. You are a Child of God and are destined for happiness, success, prosperity, love, service, peacefulness, and joy.

OCTOBER 14

"Do not be conformed to this world, but be transformed by the renewal of your mind, that by testing you may discern what is the will of God, what is good and acceptable and perfect."

— Romans 12:2

God loves you regardless of how well you are performing. The world tends to place value upon performance, title, position, wealth, and popularity. When you compare yourself with the standards of the world, it is easy to feel anxious and depressed. The world will always expect more from you. However, the good news is that your performance in the world and God's love for you are two totally separate issues. God loves you with everlasting acceptance for exactly the person you are today. In fact, there is nothing you could do today that would make God love you more. When you feel overwhelmed by the expectations of the world, rest in the loving embrace of God. In God's eyes, you are whole, complete, divine, and magnificent.

OCTOBER 15

"And rising very early in the morning,
while it was still dark, he departed and went
out to a desolate place, and there he prayed.
— Mark 1:36

Spending time in the stillness of God's presence can be challenging for you. When you make attempts at becoming silent and still, your mind tends to nag and find excuses to rush into activity. This is largely due to worldly conditioning which places value on busyness and task-prioritized accomplishments. However, *storing up your treasures in Heaven has more to do with stillness than action.*[147] God is desirous of your time and attention. Nothing you accomplish in the world could possibly make God love you more. Therefore, live close to God, and learn to bask in the warmth of His embrace. Stay with God a little bit longer today and notice the Peace of His presence.

OCTOBER 16

"Or do you not know that your body is a temple of the Holy Spirit who is in you, whom you have from God, and that you are not your own?"

— 1 Corinthians 6:19

Any thought you hold in your mind tends to evenly spread across your entire spectrum of awareness. When you worry or are fearful, your negative correlating thoughts dominate your thinking. There is simply no room left in your mind to experience the abiding comfort of God's presence. On the other hand, when you are fully joyful and abiding in the presence of God, and His love has evenly spread through your mind, there is no room left for anything except the positive correlating thoughts generated by His grace. Therefore, your first priority should always be to bring your thoughts, words, and feelings into the temple of God's presence. *Seek first the Kingdom of God, and everything else will be added to you.*[148]

OCTOBER 17

"Quickly bring out the best robe and put it on him, and put a ring on his hand and sandals on his feet."
— Luke 15:22

God is always on the lookout for you. He eagerly awaits your arrival, and rejoices every time you return to His loving presence. When you leave God's side, His heart aches for your safe return, and He thinks of you continually. Like a parent who misses their small child, God misses the time you would spend together, and counts the hours until you are back in each other's arms. When you finally return from the wayward journey of independence, God runs to meet you. He wraps His arms around you, and clothes you with His grace and mercy. *He wraps a rope of righteousness over your shoulders, and places a ring of abundance upon your hand.* Regardless of how long you were gone, God remained the same, and His love for you never changed.

OCTOBER 18

"Every athlete exercises self-control in all things. They do it to receive a perishable wreath, but we can be imperishable. So I do not run aimlessly; I do not box as one beating the air. But I discipline my body and keep it under control."

— 1 Corinthians 9:25-26

Your attention holds your awareness. Wherever your attention goes, your awareness will surely follow. Your attention breathes life into whatever it comes to focus upon. When you concentrate your attention on a thought or situation, you increase its power in your life. When you take your attention away from something, it fades out of your life. Hence the power of prayer, and the disciplined return of your attention to the presence of God. There is a momentum that is generated when you begin your day in silence and prayer. This mighty force is carried with you throughout the day, paving a path before you with goodness. Return your attention to God, and He will return His attention to you.

OCTOBER 19

"Wait for the LORD. Be strong and let your heart take courage. Yes, wait for the LORD."

— Psalm 27:14

God wants you to wait on Him with excited and hopeful anticipation for the blessings He has stored up for you. Oftentimes, you associate waiting with boredom, anxiety, and even dread. However, in spiritual realms, the experience of waiting can become a testimony of your faithfulness and trust in God. You were designed to wait on God with every fiber of your being. When you wait hopefully on God's promise to *fulfill your every need according to His riches in the glory of Christ Jesus*, you honor the assurance of His promise.[149] When you wait on God, you glorify His presence within you by showcasing your dependence on Him. *Be strong, have courage, and wait patiently on God.*

OCTOBER 20

"The mind of a sinful man is death, but the mind controlled by the Spirit is life and peace."

— Romans 8:6

The first step in establishing control of your mind is to develop control of your body. When you can direct your body to become physically still in the presence of God, your wandering mind will eventually follow suit. In the same manner that a gymnast trusts control of their body to a coach when learning a new technique, you must entrust the care of your mind to God. When you invite God to control your mind, His spirit begins to restore you from the inside out. As God continues to bless your thoughts, you will notice more and more of your time is spent thinking of things that are *right, pure, lovely, admirable, excellent, and praiseworthy.*[150]

OCTOBER 21

"I appeal to you therefore, brothers, by the mercies of God, to present your bodies as a living sacrifice, holy and acceptable to God, which is your spiritual worship."
— Romans 12:1

Your physical body is both a living testimony of God's love for you, and your expression of love for God. When you fully embrace the truth that *God is with you*, your perspective of the world will begin to change. Suddenly, nothing happens to you. Instead, you realize that everything happens for you. Your mind is elevated above the default tendency to judge things as good or bad. Everything you experience becomes a guide that is leading you closer to a relationship with God. Therefore, you must exercise the temple of your body and nourish the presence of God within you. Discipline your mind to entertain only what is good within you and the world around you. When your thoughts, words, and actions are in alignment with God, His mighty power will graciously flow through you.

OCTOBER 22

"I will instruct you and teach you in the way you should go; I will counsel you with my eye upon you."

— Psalm 32:8

Develop the discipline and sensitivity to seek God in early morning quietness. Once you make the initial connection with God, it is much easier to remain in His presence throughout your entire day. Like a trusted friend and lifetime companion, discuss everything with God. He is desirous of your communication, and is eager to assist you with every situation you encounter. As you develop *ears to hear and eyes to see*, you will find yourself in a peaceful flow with the energy of God's Universe.[151] God is both within you and slightly before you. He is preparing the path in front of you, and when you trust His leadership, the journey through the great adventure of your life becomes much more enjoyable.

OCTOBER 23

"Remember not the former things, nor consider the things of old. Behold, I am doing a new thing; now it springs forth, do you not perceive it? I will make a way in the wilderness and rivers in the desert."

— Isaiah 43:18-19

Stillness in the presence of God has the effect of a gentle ocean wave rolling upon the shore. Each time the wave's current washes over the sand, the force of the ocean draws back into itself the loose sediment and debris from the shore. The sand is left smooth and evenly dispersed. The footprints of yesterday are removed, and a blank canvas remains. The imagery of the ocean rolling over the sand is a perfect metaphor for the manner in which God is cleansing your mind of anxiety, worry, and fear. When you are silent and still in the majestic presence of God, He is able to restore your mind. The hurtful memories stored within your consciousness lose their grip over you. The path in front of you beckons, and a peaceful sense of certainty in God's plan fills your heart.

OCTOBER 24

"My heart is steadfast, O God, my heart is steadfast! I will sing and make melody!"

— Psalm 57:7

You must learn to enjoy life more. God wants you to experience the daily blessings and gifts He provides you with. When you walk around gloomy or depressed, you cut yourself off from the goodness that is right in front of you. On the other hand, when you walk through each day with positive expectancy and hopeful anticipation of God's grace, you are more able to fully receive His riches. The more you focus on God, the more He will focus on you.

OCTOBER 25

*"Ascribe to the LORD the glory due His name;
worship the LORD in the splendor of His holiness."*

— Psalm 29:2

If you focus exclusively on trying to change the past, you will experience a great deal of suffering. Every memory of your past was the result of a seed you had planted long before it occurred. The best way to deal with the past is to learn from it. When you understand your responsibility and power as a creator, everything changes. Rather than trying to change the past, your intention becomes to secure a brighter future by consciously living in the present moment. Every moment of your life is alive within the glorious presence of God. As you give yourself more and more to God, you will happily discover yourself experiencing His grace and mercy. When you free yourself of the past and hold tightly to the hand of God, you have no time for worry or regret. In the presence of God, the decisions you make today will plant the seeds for a future of heavenly proportion.

OCTOBER 26

"Come to me, all who labor and are heavy laden, and I will give you rest."

— Matthew 11:28

When a situation arises that causes you trouble, you tend to mistake the problem for your *thoughts about the problem*. The habit of your mind is to analyze, problem solve, and internally struggle against something that has already happened. Although the situation that initially caused the distress has come and gone, your mind remains trapped in the past, and continues to spin what has already happened over and over in your thinking. In these moments, God is only one breath away from calming the storm raging within your mind. Become still, and become silent. Allow God into your awareness, and focus your attention upon *His still small voice*.[152] Enjoy the peacefulness and clarity that only God can provide. Once you become still, God will guide your thinking to a heavenly perspective and light the path in front of you.

OCTOBER 27

*"Do you not know that those who run in
a race all run, but only one receives the prize?
Run in such a way that you may win."*

— 1 Corinthians 9:24

God wants you to use the strength of your mind and body in a productive way. A great athlete knows how to generate power by the productive application of their strength. Not one ounce of their strength is wasted. The lesson to be gained from great athletes is the wisdom to know what actions matter in securing victory, and what actions are a waste of energy. In order to experience the happiness, success, and prosperity God has stored up for you, first discern if you are thinking, speaking, and acting according to His Word. Bring everything before God, and allow His wisdom to guide you. Remember that you only have a finite amount of energy and willpower at your disposal each day. Therefore, learn to productively apply your strength onto what you can influence. Leave everything else in the capable hands of God.

OCTOBER 28

"But you, be strong and do not lose courage,
for there is reward for your work."

— 2 Chronicles 15:7

God wants to help you persevere. The word "perseverance" means to be steadfast in doing something despite difficulty or delay in achieving success. The character trait of perseverance is a Godly quality that is alive within you. When you set your mind on accomplishing some goal or ideal, God will lead you to its fulfillment. Your primary role is to remain persistent, and trust that in time you will be successful. Even when you face great difficulty, remain alert to God's mighty presence, and keep your eyes fixed on Him. Instead of worrying what challenges the day holds, or what tasks must be completed, focus on drawing close to God. Choose to lean on God, trusting that God will provide you the necessary strength of mind, body and spirit to persevere through this day. God is with you, and God is for you.

OCTOBER 29

"With all my heart I have sought You; Do not let me wander from Your commandments."

— Psalm 119:10

The character traits of discipline and self-control are absolutely necessary for you to achieve both spiritual and worldly success. If you desire health, happiness, and prosperity, the first step is to master your thoughts and words. If you intend a life of success, influence, purpose, and love, then you must discipline yourself to think and speak accordingly. The highest example of self-control and discipline you can follow is the life of Jesus Christ. Throw off the lesser thoughts laziness, negativity, disdain, judgment, jealousy, anger, anxiety, and fear for the greater thoughts of courage, positivity, wellness, abundance, purpose, strength and tranquility. Do not let your mind wander away from God's presence. With every ounce of your willpower, seek God and follow His ways. When you give God all of your worship and praise, God will give you all His strength and grace.

OCTOBER 30

*"For the LORD God helps me. Therefore, I am
not disgraced; I have set my face like flint,
and I know that I will not be ashamed."*

— Isaiah 50:7

God wants you to be strong and courageous and *to set your face like flint*. Flint is a very hard type of sedimentary rock. When flint is struck against steel, a spark is produced, which can result in fire. To set your face like flint implies your ability to be determined in the face of adversity. The more adverse your circumstances, the greater the reward will be for your determination. Instead of resisting or trying to avoid difficulty, learn to make friends with challenges that confront you. This is what Jesus Christ meant when he said, *"Resist not evil."*[153] When you realize that God can fit everything into a *pattern for your good*, your perspective of difficulty will begin to change.[154] Every problem and challenge can either be a stumbling block or a transforming opportunity to trust in God's great plan for your life.

OCTOBER 31

*"For where your treasure is, there your
heart will be also."*
— Matthew 6:21

Take a few moments this morning to discern where you are storing
up your treasures. Remember that all your physical possessions
belong to the world, and that you belong to God. All of your most
cherished worldly possessions will ultimately be left behind. This
perspective can help you learn the spiritual quality of thankfulness.
When you awake each day and realize that you belong to God, the
time you spend in the world takes on a lighter and gentler touch.
Self-sufficiency is an illusion that can be shattered in an instant.
Health and wealth can disappear just as easily. Instead of fearing
this hard truth, rejoice in the fragile nature of life. Learn to appreciate each moment as a gift from God. Be kind to yourself and others,
and be generous with the enduring gifts of love, forgiveness, and
goodwill.

NOVEMBER

*"We also rejoice in our sufferings, because
we know that suffering produces perseverance;
perseverance, character, and character, hope.
And hope does not disappoint us, because God
has poured out His love into our hearts by
the Holy Spirit, whom He has given us."*

— Romans 5:3-5

NOVEMBER 1

"Then the LORD God formed the man of dust from the ground and breathed into his nostrils the breath of life, and the man became a living creature."
— Genesis 2:7

When you were born, the first thing you did was take a breath. In the moments that you bring awareness to every inhale and exhale, you will experience the Peace of God. This is because every breath you take is an opportunity to be *born again in the presence of God*. Breathing creates space between your thoughts, which allows the presence of God to guide your thinking, speaking, and acting. Without space, your mind takes on the qualities of a rock with a line scratched into it. Your thoughts become habitual, and travel along the recessed path of limited awareness. However, with space between your thoughts, your mind takes on the qualities of a still body of water. As a line is drawn in the water, it immediately dissolves, and returns again to stillness. Therefore, breathe deeply today, and allow the presence of God to expand within you.

NOVEMBER 2

"The LORD is my strength and my defense; He has become my salvation. He is my God, and I will praise Him, my father's God, and I will exalt Him."

— Exodus 5:2

God is teaching you how to be strong. The qualities of determination, perseverance, strength, and courage are Christ-like. Whenever you are experiencing the contrast between feelings of weakness, and the qualities of Jesus Christ, it is because you are attempting to operate under your own capacity. Remember that God promised He would strengthen you. He did not promise that you would have the strength on your own. When you feel overwhelmed or intimidated, remember who you are: You are a child of God, and God is within you. When you allow the Light of God's presence into your circumstances, in that very moment you will be strengthened. *God is your strength and your defense.*

NOVEMBER 3

"But when you ask, you must believe and not doubt, because the one who doubts is like a wave of the sea, blown and tossed by the wind."

— James 1:6

The key to receiving the petitions of your prayers is to believe in God's infinite source of supply. If you ask God for something, and then doubt your ability to receive it, you do not doubt the object of your desire, you doubt God. And when you doubt God, you immediately cut yourself off from His universal supply. It is the same thing as tying a knot in a hose. The problem is not in the hydrant the hose is attached to, which flows freely. The problem is the knot, which prevents the water from reaching the nozzle. As soon as the knot is released, the backed-up water bursts forth with immense pressure. As a creator in God's Universe, your role is to maintain an open channel between you and God. *When you ask, believe, and prepare to receive.*

NOVEMBER 4

"Then Jesus said, 'Did I not tell you that if you believe, you will see the glory of God?'"

— John 11:40

Your ability to witness the presence of God is dependent upon your ability to believe what you cannot see. God designed you to inhabit the Holy Spirit as a felt experience, not something you can necessarily comprehend with your thinking or see with your eyes. Therefore, God is always more desirous of your feelings than of your thinking. In the same manner that you *feel love* for a spouse, child, parent, friend, or sibling, you can *feel love* for God. God does not *think* about loving you. *God feels love for you.* Every quality that enhances the intimacy of a human relationship can equally enhance your intimacy with God. You must spend an equal amount of time *feeling love for God, as you do feeling God's love for you.* To conjure up the feeling and emotion of love for God, imagine yourself embracing His Son, Jesus Christ. *It is good to be near the Lord your God.*[155]

NOVEMBER 5

"Draw near to God, and He will draw near to you."

— James 4:8

The deepest yearning of your heart is intimacy with God. This is because God designed you to seek Him above all else. The challenge for you is that God is not *out there*; no amount of external pursuit could bring Him closer to you. This is because *God is already within you*. As Jesus Christ taught, do not spend precious time *searching here, or searching there*.[156] Instead, become still in God's presence, and gently move from thinking to feeling. God is available to you in this very moment. He is simply one breath away.

NOVEMBER 6

"In the multitude of my anxieties within me, your comforts delight my soul."

— Psalm 94:9

God wants to help prepare you for this day. God is aware of every twist and turn that awaits you. Your tendency is to want to view the map of the day, or the week, or even the year that awaits you. You desire to know what lies ahead, because your mind associates knowing the future with being prepared for the future. Instead of spending precious time worrying about things that could happen in the future, *direct your attention to what is happening now.* God will not show you the road ahead. However, by spending time with God, you will be thoroughly prepared for the great adventures of your life. Whenever your mind wanders into a self-created future state, gently whisper God's name, and He will redirect your awareness to the present moment. Learn to walk upon the path of life with God, and He will guide your every step.

NOVEMBER 7

"Do not let kindness and truth leave you;
Bind them around your neck, write them
on the tablet of your heart."

— Proverbs 3:3

There is a small space between the conditions of your life and your response to them. Within this space is the peace of God. To experience His peace in any given situation, take a deep breath before responding to both the internal and external conditions of your life. Your breath will create space for God to elevate the quality of your thoughts, words, and actions.

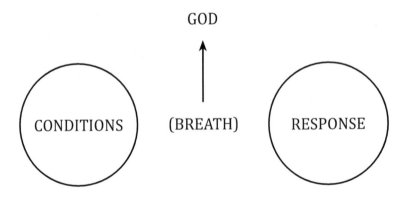

NOVEMBER 8

"Finally, brothers and sisters, whatever is true, whatever is noble, whatever is right, whatever is pure, whatever is lovely, whatever is admirable; if anything is excellent or praiseworthy, think about such things."

— Philippians 4:8

God gave you a mind and body with the intention that you would use it to worship Him. You are a magnificent temple, and just like any place of holy worship, you must keep your temple clean. One of the greatest threats against your temple is impure, evil, and negative thinking. This is why the Apostle Paul encouraged thinking about things that were *pure, lovely, noble, and righteous.* The quality of your thinking and the quality of your breathing are intimately connected. The breath is the bridge between your thinking, and your heavenly Father. Therefore, discipline yourself to take deep breaths in the presence of God. When you breathe slowly and mindfully, God joins with you, and you experience His peace. Your thoughts align with your breathing, and begin to settle. Soon, God's grace will envelop you, and His mercy will embrace your soul.

NOVEMBER 9

"Then King David went and sat before the LORD."
— 2 Samuel 7:18

When the world around you seems to spin faster and faster, it is easy to become lost in the myriad of obligations, commitments, agendas, and self-imposed priorities. As the sensations of anxiety bear down upon you, rather than trying to keep up with the world, return to the One who overcame it. There is always a calm space within you. As you return to your true center of authentic peace, you will feel safe and secure. Therefore, do not become a stranger to the presence of God. He is always standing by your side, hovering over your shoulder, and whispering words of encouragement into your ear. Allow God to fill every corner of your mind, and invite His light to shine within you.

NOVEMBER 10

"We are holding onto the hope of God's promise, which is an anchor for the soul, firm and secure."

— Hebrews 10:23

A mighty ship was being tossed about hopelessly by a raging storm. The ship remained just outside the safety of the calm and secure waters of the inner harbor, which was protected by a strong fortress-like rock formation, designed to keep the storm out. The Captain of the large ship dispatched a smaller boat from its stern to take the main anchor, and navigate through the breakers into the harbor mouth. Once there, the small boat dropped the anchor, and the larger ship was secured. This is an image of how Hope in God is an *anchor for your soul.* To be effective, you must learn to secure your life into the rock of God in the calm moments of your day. When you are connected with God, you become vibrant and radiate His love to the world. Each morning, become still in God's presence, allowing your mind to settle like a calm body of water. Then whisper, *"Help me, God"* and trust your anchor has been set.

NOVEMBER 11

*"Now faith is confidence in what we hope for
and assurance about what we do not see."*

— Hebrews 11:1

When you focus on what is ahead of you or behind you, it is easy to forget Who is *with you now*. Replaying failures or anticipating future trouble only ties up and constricts your energy. If you continue to rehearse in the theater of your mind mistakes you've made or envision future trouble, it will only increase the likelihood of its occurrence. God intended for you to only go through difficult times as *they were actually occurring*, not as they are projected across the screen of your imagination. God knew that as the difficult condition was unfolding, He would be with you. Therefore, do not multiply your suffering by holding onto regrets of the past or by planting seeds of difficulty today that will harvest tomorrow. God is with you today, and He is desirous of your attention now. He will strengthen you for the adventures of this day. Keep your eyes focused on God.

NOVEMBER 12

*"But you, man of God, flee from all this,
and pursue righteousness, godliness,
faith, love, endurance and gentleness."*

— 1 Timothy 6:11

Your frame of mind will influence the way you perceive the world around you. The same set of facts, when viewed from either a positive or negative state of mind, will be perceived in such a manner as to either bring pleasure or pain. When you view the world through the presence of God, your perspective will change in a very positive way. Problems will no longer discourage you. Instead, they will become opportunities for you to grow in faith and strength. Joyous circumstances will be magnified as you praise God for the blessings He bestowed upon you. Come to God when you are weary and burdened. Come to God when you are happy and delighted. *Allow God to be the anchor of your soul through all the days of your life.*[157]

NOVEMBER 13

*"Blessed are those who hear the
Word of God and keep it."*

— Luke 11:28

Repetition is the first law of learning. Everything you have achieved in life is the result of the repetition of certain skills that benefit you. Even the most basic of human functions, such as learning to speak and learning to walk, were achieved through thousands of repetitions. Gaining awareness and communion with God is achieved in the same manner. You must discipline yourself to repeat certain practices that draw you closer to God. Prayer, stillness, and silence in His presence are three distinct means to know God, each of which requires daily repetition in order to benefit from. Through repetition of prayer, the background music in your mind will be the Word of God. With continued stillness in His presence, a profound sense of peace will envelop you. With the cultivation of silence, the voice of God will arise from within you.

NOVEMBER 14

*"By faith we understand the universe
was formed at God's command."*

— Hebrews 11:3

When you invite God into your awareness, His presence will resonate both within you and all around you. Like a gentle breeze flowing across a still body of water, God's love will evenly fill every corner of your mind, body, and spirit.

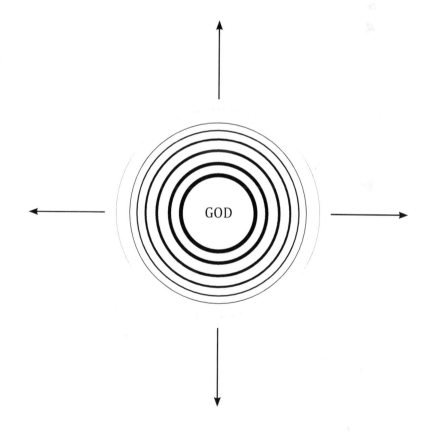

NOVEMBER 15

"By faith Abraham obeyed and went, even though he did not know where he was going."

— Hebrews 11:8

God wants you to trust His leadership with your life. It takes immense courage to abandon your own understanding, and replace it with faith in God. However, this is the type of faith God is calling you to display. When you rely on your own experience, understanding, and strength, you cut yourself off from God's unlimited supply. However, when you *trust God and obey God,* He will open the Gates of Heaven and guide your every step. *Trust in God with all your heart, and lean not on your own understanding.*[158]

NOVEMBER 16

*"Be devoted to one another in brotherly love;
give preference to one another in honor."*

— Romans 12:10

No power can deny what is already rightfully yours. God wants you to know how utterly safe and secure you are. However, in order to experience His security, you must remain within the protective embrace of His presence. The moments that you attempt to walk alone or handle trouble on your own, you limit yourself to your own strength and human understanding. Regardless of how strong you ever become, your strength pales in comparison to the strength of God. Therefore, even in moments when you perceive yourself to be faltering, continue to hold tightly to the hand of God. Have faith and trust that you are cared for, divinely protected, and intimately known by God. God is devoted to you in this moment, and all the days of your life.

NOVEMBER 17

*"You are my lamp, Oh LORD; the LORD
turns my darkness into light."*
— 2 Samuel 22:29

God wants to turn your darkness into light. When you spend time basking in the presence of God, His light will envelop you. In the presence of God, you will experience the sensation of *lightness* in two distinct ways. First, as God lifts heavy burdens from your weary shoulders, you will feel lighter and more full of energy. You realize that with God's help, you do not need to work as hard. Secondly, as God illuminates the space within your mind, the quality of your thoughts will be brightened. Your perspective will change, and you will begin to see everything through the lens of optimism and positive expectancy. As you spend time with God, He will push back the darkness around you, and fill you with His invincible light.

NOVEMBER 18

"Then Jesus spoke to them again, saying, 'I am the light of the world. He who follows me shall not walk in darkness, but have the light of life.'"

— John 8:12

Develop the ability to lean on the strength of God. The more challenging the circumstances in your life, the more strength you must draw from God. In the past, when times were troubled and difficult, your natural tendency was to rely on your own understanding and worldly capacity. However, this tactic was never quite up to the task, and you were more likely to repeat mistakes than learn from them. Therefore, starting today, have confidence in God, and trust His ability to *provide you with everything you need according to His glory and riches.*[159]

NOVEMBER 19

*"The LORD'S unfailing love surrounds
the man who trusts in Him."*

— Psalm 32:10

Remember that God is present within you each moment of your life. God's protective armor is guarding you and *His unfailing love surrounds you.* Because the world is in a constant state of flux, and the conditions in your life are always changing, it is extremely important for you to have a fixed reference point you can safely rely on. God is desirous of being the permanent rock in your life. Because *Jesus Christ is the same yesterday, today, and forever more,* you can securely ground yourself on His foundation of love, grace, and mercy.[160] Therefore, during the course of your day, continually redirect your thoughts to God. Allow His presence within you to be a source of comfort during trouble, and encouragement during challenge.

NOVEMBER 20

*"Jesus Christ is the same yesterday,
today, and forever more."*

— Hebrews 13:8

Whatever you pay attention to in your life will increase. The challenge, therefore, is for you to pay attention to what is permanent and lasting. If you only pay attention to *the fleeting desires of the world*, you will continue to be disappointed due to their impermanent nature. Each day of your life, many temptations will compete for your energy and attention. However, do not let anything compete for your attention to God. Directing your mind and heart towards God takes very little energy, and results in immense reward. The more often you consciously bring your attention to God, the stronger the connection will be. Your ability to hold the awareness of God in your mind will become the greatest blessing in your life.

NOVEMBER 21

"It is God who works in you to will and to act according to His good purpose, that you may become a child of God."

— Philippians 2:12-13

In order to make the best use of your time each day, you must determine what is important, and what is not. Once this discernment has been made, through the use of your willpower, prioritize only what is important. By continually making what is important your first priority, you will become efficient in accomplishing your dreams and goals. The key understanding here is to remember your first priority is always to *seek first the Kingdom of God.*[161] Whenever you feel distant from His presence, stop whatever you are doing and become still. No matter how challenging your circumstances, even one brief moment of stillness in the presence of God can bring immediate relief. *Trust in God at all times and pour out your heart to Him.*[162]

NOVEMBER 22

"As servants of God we commend ourselves in every way: in great endurance, in troubles, hardships and distress. Sorrowful, yet always rejoicing; poor, yet making many rich; having nothing, and yet possessing everything."

— 2 Corinthians 6:4-10

God wants to teach you the power of positive self-talk. Your ability to talk to yourself with positivity, love, and intrinsic motivation can completely change your life. You tend to rely on the encouragement of other people. However, external sources of love, support, and encouragement will never be enough to fulfill you. Only God can quench the feelings of emptiness within your heart. To develop skillful self-talk, learn to speak to yourself as if you were speaking to God. This may seem challenging at first, until you remember that the presence of God is within you. Because *God is with you*, when you speak to yourself, you are simultaneously speaking to God. As you direct thoughts of kindness, love, forgiveness, mercy, grace, and esteem to yourself, both God and you will *rejoice in the certainty that anything is possible.*

NOVEMBER 23

*"Through Christ, therefore, let us continually
offer to God a sacrifice of praise."*
— Hebrews 13:15

God created the universe in such a way that when you focus your attention upon something it will increase in your life. When you focus upon a problem, the problem will have the effect of moving closer to you. Similarly, when you focus on God, His presence will expand over your life, and His love will move closer to you. In any given moment, you have the innate ability to choose what you are focusing upon. When you focus on God during times of sadness or trouble, you are immediately lifted above your circumstances. The light of God radiates both within you and around you. Once you have focused on God, it becomes much easier to direct your mind to other thoughts that bring happiness, joy, and prosperity. Focus on God, and so that He may focus on you.

NOVEMBER 24

"I shall again praise God for the help of His presence."
— Psalm 42:5

The longer you wait to ask God for help, the more effort it will take on your part. Therefore, approach God gently each morning, and lay out your hopes, dreams, goals, prayers, and petitions for the day. Praise God for His presence within you and all around you. Enjoy the peace that only His presence can provide. You will be tempted to rush through this process, and your own understanding will encourage you to jump into the day, relying on your strength alone. You must remember that God did not create you to handle anything alone. God wants to be your partner, your friend, and your companion. *God wants to fight your battles for you.*[163] God wants to work collaboratively with you to provide everything you need.

NOVEMBER 25

"The LORD your God is with you, He is mighty to save. He will take great delight in you, He will quiet you with His love, He will rejoice over you with singing."

— Zephaniah 3:17

God takes immense delight in you. Sometimes, it is hard for you to receive compliments, praise, and love. This is because you associate your own self-worth with the quality of love you are able to receive. Remember that God loves you regardless of what you do, or fail to do. In fact, nothing you do can make God love you more. God simply wants you to relax in His presence, and receive the abundant love He has stored up for you. Every moment of your life you can choose to focus on your circumstances, or to focus on God. Even in the midst of important events, you can remain aware of the presence of God. As you grow in faith, the quiet time you spend with God will become your first priority.

NOVEMBER 26

*"The LORD makes His face to shine upon and
enlighten you and be gracious to you."*

— Numbers 6:25

Spend more time with God today than you did yesterday. The world, with its continual demands for your attention, can be put on hold. Sadly, many times you put God on hold, rationalizing that you do not have enough time to be still in His presence. The longer you push God into the background of your life, the more challenging it will be to feel His constant presence. Take delight in the fact that God is always closer than you think. His love is richly present in every moment of your life. Ask God to open your eyes and heart to His tender presence. Although it is easy to feel connected to what your eyes can see, real peace can only be achieved by connecting with what your heart can feel. *Faith is the confirmation of things you do not see, perceiving as real what is not revealed to your senses.*[164]

NOVEMBER 27

*"The eyes of the LORD are on those who fear Him,
on those whose hope is in His unfailing love."*

— Psalm 33:18

To "fear God" has nothing to do with being afraid of punishment or having feelings of anxiousness. *Fearing God is in fact the beginning of wisdom.*[165] To fear God means to be concerned of displeasing the One who unconditionally loves and adores you. Like a child who does not want to displease their parent, God wants you to have a personal intimacy with Him unlike any worldly relationship you have ever known. God is your greatest source of security, love, and hope. Rejoice in the certainty that *God's loving eyes are upon you.*

NOVEMBER 28

"Now may the Lord of peace Himself give you peace at all times and in every way."

— Romans 8:38

When Jesus Christ said, *"Do not worry about tomorrow,"* he was not making a mere suggestion, but rather a strong command.[166] God divided time into days and nights, so that you would have manageable portions of life to handle. Within this manageable segment of each day, God promised that His grace would be sufficient for you. However, you must remember that His sufficiency is only enough for one day at a time. Although God is the *everlasting God*, He is only able to meet you in the present moments of your life. When you become still with your thoughts, you will realize that anxiety tends to live in the future, and regret tends to live in the past. The insertion point for God to enter your life is in the present moment. As you direct your awareness to God, you effortlessly slip into the present, and the shackles of anxiety and regret fall from your shoulders.

NOVEMBER 29

"Though you have not seen Him, you love Him; though you do not see Him now, you believe in Him and are filled with an inexpressible and glorious joy."

— 1 Peter 1:7-8

There is a difference between seeking peace in God, and peace in the world. Seeking peace in the world is dependent upon people, conditions, and material possessions. To seek peace in the world causes you frustration and anxiety, because any peace you happen across is fleeting and temporary. It is a slippery slope to seek comfort in the world. Your attention tends to be drawn towards what you can see and hold in hand. True peace and permanent joy, however, can only be found in *what you will not see and cannot touch*. Therefore, instead of seeking peace in the world, find comfort in the Prince of Peace, and the One who overcame the world. Regardless of the torrent a storm may produce, the sky will return to blue, and the sun will shine again. Adverse conditions will come and go in the same manner. God is always the same, and His peace is always a safe place for your soul.

NOVEMBER 30

*"The eternal God is your refuge, and
underneath are His everlasting arms."*
— Deuteronomy 33:27

You will not find peace by engaging in excessive planning, or attempting to control what will happen to you in the future. In fact, seeking to control future events is a form of unbelief, because you are not trusting God's ability to provide everything you need. When your mind spins with multiple plans and future scenarios, the illusion of peace may tempt you, and you might think it is just within your grasp. However, just when you think you have prepared for everything and all possibilities, something unexpected will throw you back into confusion and suffering. Remember that God did not design your mind to foresee the future. God designed your mind to rejoice in the present moment. God created your mind for continual communication and awareness of His presence, which you can only behold in the present moment. Therefore, *commit everything into the care of God, and He will make your paths prosperous.*[167]

DECEMBER

*"Lean on, trust in, and be confident in the LORD
with all your heart and mind and do not lean
on your own insight or understanding."*

— Proverbs 3:5

DECEMBER 1

*"Come to Me, all who labor and are
heavy laden, and I will give you rest."*

— Matthew 11:28

God wants you to take rest in His peaceful presence. Because God is eternal and everlasting, you can escape into the peace of His presence at anytime. In your current spiritual practice, you are able to spend small amounts of time with God, especially when things are going well. However, God wants you to trust in Him at all times, and under all conditions. God wants your attention throughout every waking moment of your day. Whenever you feel unstable or troubled by your circumstances, remember that your footing is always assured when you walk with God. The strength of God is more than enough to bear any burden you might be carrying. Remember these three promises of God: *Any challenge you face will be overcome.*[168] *No obstacle shall stand in your way.*[169] *All your needs will be provided.*[170]

DECEMBER 2

"But as for me, I will look to the LORD; I will wait for the God of my salvation; my God will hear me."

— Micah 7:7

God wants you to feel the joy and positive expectancy only His presence can provide. In order to accomplish this, you must develop the felt experience of *joyfully waiting for the Lord.*[171] Like a child whose excitement increases as a birthday approaches, God wants you to live in such a way that enthusiasm and joyful expectation become your center point. As you become more vigilant and determined to experience the presence of God, He will take note and reward your efforts. Trust that God will hear every word you say, and see every action you take. *Today is the day the Lord has made.*[172] Seek God today with all your strength.

DECEMBER 3

"More than that, we rejoice in our sufferings, knowing that suffering produces endurance, and endurance produces character, and character produces hope."

— Romans 5:3-4

Great athletes know what it means to suffer, and come to value the experience the sensation provides. In races of high intensity and long endurance, oftentimes the winner is the athlete who was able to withstand the most agonizing amount of suffering. God wants you to understand that when you experience difficulty, challenge, and suffering, the benefits will far outweigh *the light and momentary trouble.*[173] Develop the frame of mind that everything that happens to you is making you stronger. Create mental space between what arises in your awareness and your reaction to it. When you are able to release all emotional attachment to your circumstances, you will understand what Jesus Christ meant when he said, *"Sell all you have and distribute it to the poor. Then come and follow me."*[174]

DECEMBER 4

"You, my brothers and sisters, were called to be free. But do not use your freedom to indulge the flesh; rather, serve one another humbly in love."

— Galatians 5:13

God made you with a unique purpose to fulfill during your brief time on earth. Although you tend to identify with your physical body, you are in fact a spiritual being. Therefore, your unique life purpose has more to do with *who you are than what you do.* Each experience of your life is like a roadmap that is ultimately leading you home to your authentic spiritual self. This is the deeper meaning of the Scripture, *"Your God shall supply all your need, according to His riches in the glory of Christ Jesus."*[175] When you realize that your life experiences are intended to help you discover your innate divine nature, you will have taken a giant leap in self-awareness and God-consciousness. In order to begin the process of identifying with your spiritual self, focus more on serving other people than yourself.

DECEMBER 5

"Before I formed you in the womb I knew you, and before you were born I consecrated you; I appointed you a prophet to the nations."

— Jeremiah 1:5

When you take joy in the service of others, you will experience the bliss of Jesus Christ's commandment, *"Love one another."*[176] You were born with unique talents and even more unique ways of expressing them. When you embrace God's presence within you, identify with your unique talents, and then use those talents in the service of others, you will experience true prosperity. Your life will take on a miraculous quality, and success will find you wherever you go. Ask God to illuminate your heart and help you uncover your great talents, and unique gift to the world. As you travel through the adventures of this day, find as many occasions as possible to express your gifts and talents. *As you give, so shall you receive. The measure you use will be measured back to you.*[177]

DECEMBER 6

*"I cry out to God most high, to God
who fulfills His purpose for me."*

— Psalm 57:2

When you praise God for the desires of your heart, the fulfillment of that desire is magnetized into your life in seemingly miraculous fashion. The testimony of your faith in God is measured before you receive, not afterwards. This is the meaning of the Scripture, *"Whatever you pray for, believe that you have received it, and it shall be yours."*[178] Whatever you desire is within your capacity to achieve, acquire, and hold in hand. With a heart like Jesus Christ, praise God for your desires, and with positive expectancy, eagerly await their arrival.

DECEMBER 7

"Arise, for it is your task, and we are with you; be strong and do it."

— Ezra 10:4

The voices of the world tend to compete for your attention with your higher spiritual self. Instead of listening to the voices of the world, challenge them by speaking the Word of God. Each time you consciously speak the Word of God, either in the privacy of your mind or out loud, you effectively take a mini-break from the world. In these precious breaks, you shift from the external gravitational pull on your attention to the inward presence of God. There is a great treasure of peace you can discover in the Word of God. Although God is continually pouring His blessings out to you, some of His richest treasures must be actively sought. As you speak God's Word, His presence is revealed to you more and more. *Ask and it will be given to you; seek and you will find; knock and the door will be opened for you.*[179]

DECEMBER 8

*"So teach us to number our days that
we may get a heart of wisdom."*
— Psalm 90:12

The best way to become aware of the seeds you are planting into the fertile soil of God's Universe is to become conscious of every decision you make. Whether you like it or not, everything you are experiencing in this moment is a result of seeds you have planted in the past. Unfortunately, many of these choices were made without conscious awareness. Nevertheless, God's Universe retains a perfect accounting system: Over time, you will be responsible for every thought, word, and action you produce. The best way to ensure the fruit of your future harvest will benefit you is to develop conscious awareness of your current decisions. In the small space between every condition of your life, and your reaction to it, is perfect happiness and ultimate peace. Invite the presence of God into this space, and ask His spirit to guide your thinking, speaking, and acting.

DECEMBER 9

"One gives freely, yet grows all the richer; another withholds what he should give, and only suffers want. Whoever brings blessing will be enriched, and one who waters will himself be watered."

— Proverbs 11:24-25

Success in life could be defined as your continued expansion of happiness and the progressive realization of worthy goals. The greatest goal and ultimate source of happiness is your aware-ness of God's presence within you. When your heart awakens to the presence of God, every worldly desire will effortlessly become available to you. As you align yourself with the Word of God, you align yourself with His Universe. Your source of happiness will shift from the transient desires of the world, to the permanent treasures of Heaven. You will realize the divinity within yourself, and each person you encounter. Spend more time today with God than you did yesterday. Remain aware of His loving presence both within you and all around you. *Your body is a temple for the spirit of God within you.*[180]

DECEMBER 10

*"If a house is divided against itself,
that house cannot stand."*

— Mark 3:25

You are continually drawing into your life what you give and expect. Whether you attract good or bad, it is determined by this same principle. Reflect on how often you have either said or heard another person comment, *"This is just what I expected."* Oftentimes, you invite the condition you either desire or fear based simply on your continual thinking about it. Therefore, it is absolutely vital you discipline yourself to think about *whatever is pure, whatever is lovely, whatever is admirable, whatever is excellent and whatever is praiseworthy.*[181] In addition to thinking positively, it is equally important that you expect to achieve what you are thinking about. Ensure you are not thinking one thing, while expecting another. This is why Jesus Christ taught, *"A house divided against itself cannot stand."* When you feel certainty in your heart that you will achieve the desires of your mind, the great blessings God has stored up will be yours.

DECEMBER 11

"The point is this: Whoever sows sparingly will also reap sparingly, and whoever sows bountifully, will also reap bountifully. Each one must give as he has decided in his heart, not reluctantly or under compulsion, for God loves a cheerful giver."

— 2 Corinthians 9:6-7

You cannot feel a desire that you are not ready and able to achieve. The mere fact the desire arises in your consciousness is proof you are capable of obtaining it. The true desires of your heart represent God's love expressing itself through you. Your prayers, desires, and your inner longing for expression are like a magnet, and the stronger the attraction, the stronger your ability to obtain whatever you want. However, in all matters of your heart's desires, you can only obtain what you are prepared to give. Identify the feeling that would result form achieving whatever you desire, and then find a way to give that feeling away. Remember to always give with a free and willing spirit. When you give of your love, time, energy, and kindness, it will come back to you with compounded interest.

DECEMBER 12

"Blessed is the man who endures temptation, for when he is tried he shall receive the crown of life, which the Lord has promised to them that love Him."

— James 1:12

Many voices compete for your attention, time, and energy. It will be impossible for you to obtain your ambitions until you are able to resist these worldly temptations. In order to truly experience your spiritual nature, your mind and ideals must be in harmony with God. Everything in life has its own price. This principle is called the Law of Sacrifice, and states that something always has to be scarified for something else. You are sacrificing every day of your life, whether you realize it or not. No matter what you desire out of life, you must give something up in order to achieve it. Therefore, ensure you are giving up something of lesser value for something of greater value. Adhere to these three points:

1. God is desirous of your time and attention.

2. God is the greatest value.

3. Give your time and attention to God.

DECEMBER 13

"Give, and it will be given to you. Good measure, pressed down, shaken together, running over, will be put into your lap. For with the measure you use it will be measured back to you."

— Luke 6:38

Giving and receiving are two sides of the same coin. God's Universe operates through dynamic exchange. Nothing in the world is static or without change. Oftentimes, you experience pain and suffering by your vain attempts to keep things as they are. The only thing you will ever experience in your life that is *the same today, yesterday and tomorrow* is the presence of God.[182] As you give more of your time to God, your ability to receive His presence and love will increase. The word "affluence" comes from the root word "affluere" which means "to flow to." As you direct your awareness and give your attention to God, His love will effortlessly flow into your life. The desires of your heart will flow into your life as well, for God promised *seek first the Kingdom of God, and everything else will be added to you.*[183]

DECEMBER 14

"Therefore let us draw near with confidence to the throne of grace, so that we may receive mercy and find grace to help in time of need."

— Hebrews 4:16

A father asked his son to move a large rock. The young boy struggled under the tremendous weight of the stone. He tugged, pushed, lifted, and wrestled the stone with little success. The young boy asked his friends to help, but still the rock would not budge.

Finally, in despair, the young boy went to his father and said,

"Dad, I've tried everything, but I can't move the rock."

"Have you done all you could?" asked the father.

"Yes, I've done everything I could think of to move the rock," said the boy.

"Son, you have not yet done everything," replied his father, *"For you haven't asked me for help."*

DECEMBER 15

"Every man shall give as he is able, according to the blessing of the LORD your God that He has given you."
— Deuteronomy 16:17

Discipline your mind to crowd out all negative thoughts by positive thoughts, evil thoughts by kind thoughts, ugly thoughts by beautiful thoughts, and distressing thoughts by pleasant thoughts. As you begin to think more superior thoughts, you will start to overcome the growth of confused states of mind and negative perception. God is teaching you to think of all conditions, all events, all persons, and all circumstances from the ideal point of view and highest perspective. As you receive His strength and continually align with His presence, your entire existence will transform for the better. As you mentally discipline yourself to look for the good, the good will look for you. As you begin to form higher conceptions of the good, the elements of good will find their expression in your thoughts, words, and actions. With all your heart and all your strength, seek the presence of God. As your life draws close to God, His love will draw close to you.

DECEMBER 16

*"Blessed be the God and Father of our Lord
Jesus Christ, who has blessed us in Christ with
every spiritual blessing in the heavenly places."*

— Ephesians 1:3

Every thought you think is like a magnetic force sent out into God's Universe, which begins the process of drawing back onto itself like conditions. Therefore, whatever your current position in life might be, before you can hope to receive any measure of increased success, you must discipline yourself to control your magnetic thought forces. As you cultivate a calm, disciplined, and loving mindset, God's presence will expand within and around you. Through the strength of God, every difficulty you face, however great or seemingly impossible, will yield before you. Through the concentrated use of your mind, every desire of your heart will be speedily attracted to you. Think good thoughts, and they will quickly become actualized in the outward conditions, circumstances, and events of your life. *You shall accomplish that which you propose, and succeed in the thing for which you were sent.*[184]

DECEMBER 17

"So shall my word be that goes out from my mouth; it shall not return to me empty, but it shall accomplish that which I propose, and shall succeed in the thing for which I sent it."

— Isaiah 55:11

Whatever you would hope to become in life, you can become in this very moment. Non-accomplishment and non-achievement are the result of your perpetual postponement and procrastination. Because you have the power to postpone, you also have the power to accomplish and immediately materialize. When this powerful truth is understood and applied in your life, you will be today and every day the ideal person you have long dreamed of. The creative power to design the life of your dreams resides in your speaking and thinking. Ask the spirit of God to fill you with His authority, and then say to yourself, *"I can do all things through Christ who strengthens me. Whatever I say, and whatever I do, will succeed."*[185]

DECEMBER 18

*"The light shines in the darkness, and
the darkness has not overcome it."*

— John 1:5

In God's great Universe, darkness is like a passing shadow, and light is the substance that remains. Darkness is temporary, and light is permanent. Similarly, in the vast universe of your mind, of which the universe of God takes residence, sorrow is fleeting, but joy remains forever. No true thing can pass away, and no false thing can be preserved. Sorrow is false and cannot live forever. Joy is true and cannot pass away. When the sun is temporarily hidden behind a passing cloud, you remain certain that it will shine again. Similarly, joy may be hidden for a time, but trust that it too will always be recovered. Joy will transcend sorrow, as light will transcend darkness. Light and joy are your divine birthright. You are a magnificent child of God. Never think that your sorrow, trouble, or difficulty will remain, for God promised they will pass like a cloud. Rejoice in the presence and light of God, which shines in you and all around you.

DECEMBER 19

"I will turn the darkness before them into light, the rough places into level ground. These are the things I do, and I do not forsake them."

— Isaiah 42:16

The conditions of your life can affect you only so far as your thinking allows them to do so. You have the ability to assign power to anything you think about. If a condition arises in your awareness, and you label it as negative, it will affect you in a negative way. Even though the good of every seemingly bad condition eagerly awaits your perception, you will not be able to behold it. Until you develop the ability to control your thinking, the conditions of your life will toss you about. However, in the moment you regain control of your mind and elevate the quality of your thinking, the way before you will be prosperous, and success will be yours. No condition or event shall ever possess power over the constructive use of your mind. *The Kingdom of Heaven is within you, and no sadness can enter therein.*[186]

DECEMBER 20

"This Book of the Law shall not depart from your mouth, but you shall meditate on it day and night, so that you may be careful to do according to all that is written in it. For then you will make your way prosperous, and then you will have good success."

— Joshua 1:8

When you become silent in the peaceful presence of God, your mind takes on the qualities of a still body of water. As you focus your mind upon God, every cell within your body opens to receive His healing light. Stillness and silence in the presence of God is the very essence of prayer. When you become still in the presence of God, your soul reaches up for the hand of God. Physical stillness in your body allows for the intense use of your mind to focus upon God with the intention of feeling His presence within you, and all around you. Over time, you will become what you think about. Therefore, think about God. Allow His presence to radiate through you, and hold the feeling of His love in your heart at all times.

DECEMBER 21

"I will meditate on your precepts
and fix my eyes on your ways."
— Psalm 119:15

Discipline yourself to continually turn your attention inward to the presence of God in you. Although the outward gravitational pull of the world is tempting, with diligent practice your attention can remain fixed on God.

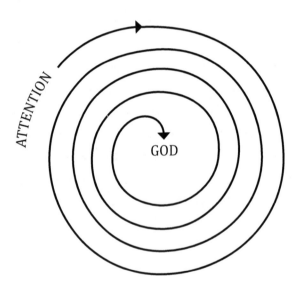

DECEMBER 22

"His delight is in the Law of the LORD, and on His Law he meditates day and night. He is like a tree planted by streams of water that yields its fruit in its season, and its leaf does not wither. In all that he does, he prospers."

— Psalm 1:2-3

Your must discipline yourself to think exclusively of what you desire, as opposed to the absence of it. This principle is known as the Law of Attraction, and to abide by it is to live in harmony with God's Universe. To think of what you desire can be explained in the following example: If you were cold, you would not work with cold in order to get warm. You would build a fire, draw near to it, and enjoy the warmth the heat from the fire provided. As you built up the warmth, the cold would disappear, for cold is the absence of heat. Therefore, think about what you desire, and the lack of it will disappear from your life. Think about health, purity, loveliness, kindness, prosperity, and peacefulness. Hold strongly to the truth that God's intention for you is *goodness and love all the days of your life.*[187]

DECEMBER 23

"Draw near to God, and He will draw near to you."
— James 4:8

Jesus Christ used the metaphor of *reaping what you sow* in order to explain the karmic implications of our thoughts, words, and actions. Over time, you will become what you think about. Therefore, you must learn to begin right each morning by connecting with the presence of God. When you spend time thinking of God, you draw more of His presence and power into your life. Once the connection with God is made, it is much easier for your thinking to come into alignment with ideas and concepts of love, prosperity, and goodness. As God becomes the set-point of your mind, your ability to attract good conditions into your life will increase by epic proportion. Even seemingly troubling conditions will be viewed from their highest perspective, and you will experience good through them. Always remember that whatever you are focusing on is also focusing on you. *Focus on God, so that He may focus on you.*

DECEMBER 24

"My sheep hear my voice, and I know them, and they follow me. I give them eternal life, and they will never perish, and no one will snatch them out of my hand. My Father, who has given them to me, is greater than all, and no one is able to snatch them out of the Father's hand. I and the Father are one."

— John 10:27-30

Spend the majority of your time today in prayer and communion with God. Unlike a human relationship in which communication is expressed through the action of touch and speech, communion with God can happen in the silence of your heart. Develop the discipline to steal away quiet moments with God during the course of your day. Even one mindful breath can be an anchor to your soul, bringing your awareness back to the presence of God. Revel in the felt experience of receiving God's embrace, which is surrounding you at all times and places. The more you direct your thoughts and feelings to God, the more He will direct His thoughts and feelings towards you. With diligent practice, you will come to understand the meaning of Christ's statement, *"I and the Father are one."*

DECEMBER 25

"To the pure, all things are pure."
— Titus 1:15

You will attract into your life what you spend the majority of your time thinking about. Any thought or statement continually repeated, along with the compounding effect of emotion and feeling, will materialize into your reality. The potential dangers with unconscious thought and speech patterns are they can become a habit in your life. A fully formed habit can be so powerful that decisions are made without your conscious awareness. This is the reason stillness and silence in the presence of God is so important for you. When you become still in the loving embrace of God, His grace will lift you from the depths of self-destructive habits of thinking and speaking that no longer serve you. In the light of His mercy, deep-rooted habits of negativity, self-doubt, insecurity, and fear will melt away. Your mind will be like an empty cup, ready to receive God's glorious supply of faith, hope, love, positivity, and encouragement. Allow God to give you the gift of His peace.

DECEMBER 26

"And He said to them, 'Pay attention to what you hear; with the measure you use, it will be measured to you, and still more will be added. For to the one who has, more will be given.'"

— Mark 4:24

The thoughts you give life and energy to will become your feelings and emotions. Your feelings and emotions act like a strong magnet, attracting similar circumstances, events, people, and ultimately an entire reality, which will then perfectly match the original thoughts you had energized. This is why Jesus Christ taught that *out of the abundance of your heart an entire reality would be shaped.*[188] One of the best ways to establish a feeling of peacefulness, love, contentment, and abundance is to spend time alone with God. Turn your attention inward, close your eyes, and become still. Gradually, the turmoil of your mind will calm, and God's love will envelop you. God will elevate the quality of your thinking. Your good thoughts will attract more good thoughts. *Seek first the Kingdom of God, and everything else will be added to you.*[189]

DECEMBER 27

"In the same way, even though we are many individuals, Christ makes us one body and individuals who are connected to each other."

— Romans 12:5

One morning, a young man was walking along the beach after a storm. The young man noticed all the seaweed and debris that had washed up on the shore, and thought it was the worst storm he had ever seen.

Up ahead in the distance, the young man saw what appeared to be someone dancing in the waves. As he drew near, he observed an old man was picking up starfish, and throwing them back into the sea.

"What are you doing, old man?" asked the young man.

"I am saving the lives of all these starfish," the old man replied.

"You can't possible make a difference," said the young man, *"There are thousands of starfish on the beach!"*

The old man picked up a starfish, and with all his strength, threw it far into the ocean.

"It made a difference to that one," he said.

DECEMBER 28

*"Set your minds on things that are above,
not on things that are on the Earth."*

— Colossians 3:2

God gave you a mind and body with the intention that you would use it to worship Him. Your mind is like a magnificent temple, and just like any place of holy worship, you must keep your temple clean. Therefore, you must learn to discipline *the way you look at things*. When you change the way you look at something, what you look at begins to change. In the world around you, there are both magnificent vistas of beauty, as well as dark wastelands. Condition yourself to look for the beauty in every situation. When you focus on *whatever is true, righteous, and lovely,* you will find hope, encouragement, and strength.[190] God created you with the ability to enjoy beauty, wellness, goodness, and prosperity. When you focus on these qualities, your soul is blessed, and your heart is open to the presence of God.

DECEMBER 29

"A thousand may fall at your side, and ten thousand at your right hand; but it shall not come near you."

— Psalm 91:7

You are protected and surrounded by the sword and shield of God. No challenge, opposition, or worldly trouble will ever defeat you, for you are a child of God. Therefore, approach problems with a gentle touch and sense of peaceful security. God is with you, God is for you, and *God is fighting your battles for you.*[191] Any form of worry is a lack of trust in the great plan and adventure God has in store for you. Enter into each day with the courage of ten thousand mighty warriors. Have the confidence that God will protect you, vindicate you, and overcome all obstacles before you.

DECEMBER 30

"No power in the sky above or in the earth below—indeed, nothing in all creation will ever be able to separate us from the love of God."

— Romans 8:39

Nothing you do could ever separate you from God's loving embrace. Everywhere you go, the presence of God remains with you. Even during the darkest nights, the light of God still shines. Many worldly relationships are based on the principle of *cause and effect*. Things you do are either liked or disliked by other people. However, God's love for you transcends reason and human understanding. Nothing you do, or fail to do, has a bearing on God's love for you. God loves you for the person you have been, the person you are now, and the person you will be tomorrow. God's love for you is unconditional, everlasting, and eternal. Rest with confidence in God's love, and take comfort in relinquishing the need to perform. Spend less time *doing* and more time *being a child of God*.

DECEMBER 31

"Let all bitterness and wrath and anger and clamor and slander be put away from you, along with all malice. Be kind to one another, tenderhearted, forgiving one another, as God in Christ forgave you."

— Ephesians 4:31-32

Jesus Christ said, *"Seek first the Kingdom of God, and everything else will be added to you."*[192] Heaven is not a far away place, available to you only upon death. Heaven is a state of mind, available for you to enter into now. To enter God's Kingdom and develop a heart like Christ, you must first align your thinking with the mind of God. To gain intimacy with God and a heart like His Son, you must discipline yourself to maintain a positive, constructive, and orderly state of thinking. Whatever dominant thought is held in your mind will become your reality. Therefore, *pray continually and at all times that you would experience the presence of God.*[193] You are a divine child of God, and your birthright is to know Him as a friend, father, and redeemer. *May the peace of God be with you at the end of this year, and at the beginning of the next.*

ALSO FROM BESTSELLING AUTHOR GREG AMUNDSON

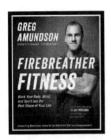

Greg Amundson's effective guides to functional fitness, nutrition, goal-setting, pain tolerance, honing purpose and focus, and exerting control over your mental state are designed to help meet any challenge. Packed with practical advice, vetted training methods, and Amundson's guided workout programs, *Firebreather Fitness* is a must-have resource for athletes, coaches, law enforcement and military professionals, and anyone interested in pursuing the high-performance life. Includes a foreword from *New York Times* bestselling author Mark Divine.

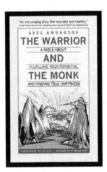

The Warrioir and The Monk tells the extraodinary story of a young warrior who seeks the counsel of a wise monk on the universal quest to find true happiness. This is Greg Amundson's #1 Amazon multi-category bestselling book.

ABOUT THE AUTHOR

GREG AMUNDSON is among the nation's forefront authorities on integrated wellness. A former DEA Special Agent, SWAT Operator, and Army Captain turned Kokoro Yoga Instructor, Krav Maga Black Belt, and Masters of Divinity Graduate Student, Greg's message will help you internalize disciplined practices that are central to developing a relationship with  God. His integration of the Mind, Body, and Spirit offers a unique perspective to keep you thriving in all aspects of your life. For more information, visit www.GregoryAmundson.com.

KEYNOTES AND SEMINARS

Greg Amundson is one of North America's most electric, encouraging, and motivating professional speakers. Greg has logged more than 10,000 hours of dynamic public speaking on topics including leadership, intrinsic motivation, holistic wellness practices, functional fitness, warrior spirit, and God's Love. Greg speaks around the Country to Law Enforcement Departments on integrating disciplined warrior practices to foster increased Officer Safety while simultaneously generating stronger community relationships. A plank owner of the highly regarded Eagle Rise Speaker Bureau, Greg is renowned for his ability to transcend boundaries and speak to the heart of Spirituality. His use of captivating storytelling results in a profound and transformational learning experience.

To book Greg Amundson at your next conference or in-house event please visit www.GregoryAmundson.com.

INDEX

JANUARY

[1] These ideas were shaped in my mind through the work of James Allen in his book *As A Man Thinketh* (Dover Publications, 2007).

[2] The account of Jesus raising Lazarus from the dead may be further studied in John 11:38-43.

[3] The account of Elijah praying for rain may be further studied in 1 Kings 18:16-46.

[4] In Mathew 11:24, Jesus Christ said, "Therefore I tell you, whatever you ask for in prayer, believe that you have received it, and it will be yours."

[5] In Matthew 7:7, Jesus Christ said, "Ask and it will be given to you; seek and you will find; knock and the door will be opened to you."

[6] In Matthew 23:37-38, Jesus Christ explained the greatest commandment when he said, "To love the Lord your God with all your heart and with all your soul and with all your mind. This is the first and greatest commandment."

[7] In Matthew 7:24-27, Jesus Christ taught the parable of the Wise and Foolish Builders. He said, "Everyone who hears these words of mine and puts them into practice is like a wise man who build his house on the rock. The rain came down, the streams rose, and the winds blew and beat against that house; yet it did not fall, because it had its foundation on the rock."

[8] In Luke 17:21, Jesus Christ said, "The Kingdom of God is within you."

[9] In James 1:17, James wrote that, "Every good and perfect gift comes down from the Father." James was the half-brother of Jesus, and learned this principle firsthand from him.

[10] In Mark 11:24, Jesus Christ said, "Whatever you ask for in prayer, believe that you have received it, and it will be yours."

[11] "Do not be deceived: God cannot be mocked. A man reaps what he sows. Whoever sows to please their flesh, from the flesh will reap destruction; whoever sows to please the Spirit, from the Spirit will reap eternal life" (Galatians 6:7-8).

[12] "'Don't be afraid,'" the prophet answered. 'Those who are with us are more than those who are with them'" (2 Kings 6:16).

FEBRUARY

[13] In Matthew 6:19-20, Jesus Christ said, "Do not store up for yourselves treasures on earth, where moths and vermin destroy, and where thieves break in and steal. But store up for yourselves treasures in heaven, where moths and

vermin do not destroy, and where thieves do not break in and steal. For where your treasure is, there your heart will be also."

14 "Be still and know I am God. I will be exalted among all the nations. I will be exalted in the earth" (Psalm 46:10).

15 "Create within me a clean heart, O God, and put a new and right spirit within me" (Psalm 51:10).

16 "Surely your goodness and love will follow me all the days of my life, and I will dwell in the house of the LORD forever" (Psalm 23:6).

17 "But when you pray, go into your room, close the door and pray to your Father, who is unseen. Then your Father, who sees what is done in secret, will reward you" (Matthew 6:6).

18 These ideas were shaped in my mind through the work of James Allen in his book *As A Man Thinketh* (Dover Publications), 2007.

19 "Yet for us there is but one God, the Father, from whom all things came and for whom we live; and there is but one Lord, Jesus Christ, through whom all things came and through whom we live" (1 Corinthians 8:6).

20 "Finally, brothers and sisters, whatever is true, whatever is noble, whatever is right, whatever is pure, whatever is lovely, whatever is admirable — if anything is excellent or praiseworthy — think about such things" (Philippians 4:8).

21 "Surely your love and goodness will follow me all the days of my life, and I will dwell in the house of the LORD forever" (Psalm 23:6).

22 "Seek first the Kingdom of God and His righteousness and everything else will be added to you" (Matthew 6:6).

23 "With God all things are possible" (Matthew 19:26).

24 "In Christ I can do all things" (Philippians 4:13).

25 "Or take ships as an example. Although they are so large and are driven by strong winds, they are steered by a very small rudder wherever the pilot wants to go" (James 3:4).

26 "Surely your love and goodness will follow me all the days of my life, and I will dwell in the house of the LORD forever" (Psalm 23:6).

27 "'Don't be afraid,'" the prophet answered. 'Those who are with us are more than those who are with them'" (2 Kings 6:16).

28 "Do not be afraid of them; the LORD your God himself will fight for you" (Deuteronomy 3:22).

29 This idea was formed in my mind through the work of B.K.S. Iyengar in his book, *Light on Life: The Yoga Journey to Wholeness, Inner Peace, and Ultimate Freedom* (Iyengar Yoga Books), September 19, 2006.

[30] "You prepare a table before me in the presence of my enemies. You anoint my head with oil; my cup overflows. Surely your goodness and love will follow me all the days of my life, and I will dwell in the house of the LORD forever" (Psalm 23:5-6).

[31] In John 16:24, Jesus Christ said, "Ask and you shall receive, that your joy may be complete."

[32] This idea was shaped in my mind through the work of Dr. Deepak Chopra in his book *The Seven Spiritual Laws of Success*, (New World Library / Amber-Allen Publishing), November 9, 1994.

[33] "And my God will meet all your needs according to the riches of his glory in Christ Jesus" (Philippians 4:19).

[34] "But seek first the Kingdom of God and His righteousness, and all these things will be added to you" (Matthew 6:33).

[35] The reference to becoming still in the presence of God and listening to *"His still small voice"* are interpreted from the verse, "After the earthquake came a fire, but the Lord was not in the fire. And after the fire came a gentle whisper" (1 Kings 19:12) and Psalm 46:10, "Be still, and know that I am God."

MARCH

[36] In Matthew 15:19, Jesus Christ said, "For out of the heart come evil thoughts—murder, adultery, sexual immorality, theft, false testimony, slander."

[37] "God and Father of all, who is over all and through all and in all" (Ephesians 4:6)

[38] "Now to him who is able to do immeasurably more than all we ask or imagine, according to his power that is at work within us" (Ephesians 3:20).

[39] "I can do all things through Christ who strengthens me" (Philippians 4:13).

[40] "Those who hope in the LORD will renew their strength. They will soar on wings like eagles; they will run and not grow weary, they will walk and not be faint" (Isaiah 40:31).

[41] "Jesus Christ is the same yesterday and today and forever" (Hebrews 13:8).

[42] This idea was formed in my mind through the work of B.K.S. Iyengar in his book, *Light on Life: The Yoga Journey to Wholeness, Inner Peace, and Ultimate Freedom* (Iyengar Yoga Books), September 19, 2006.

[43] This idea was formed in my mind through the work of B.K.S. Iyengar in his book, *Light on Life: The Yoga Journey to Wholeness, Inner Peace, and Ultimate Freedom* (Iyengar Yoga Books), September 19, 2006.

[44] "Draw near to God and He will draw near to you" (James 4:8).

⁴⁵ "The LORD your God is with you, the mighty warrior who saves. He will take great delight in you; in His love he will no longer rebuke you, but will rejoice over you with singing" (Zephaniah 3:17).

⁴⁶ In Matthew 6:33, Jesus Christ said, "Seek first the Kingdom of God and His righteousness, and everything else will be added to you."

⁴⁷ "The LORD is my shepherd, I shall not want" (Psalm 23:1).

⁴⁸ "And we know that all things work together for good for those who love God" (Romans 8:28).

⁴⁹ "Those who hope in the LORD will renew their strength. They will soar on wings like eagles; they will run and not grow weary, they will walk and not be faint" (Isaiah 40:31).

⁵⁰ "Surely goodness and love will follow me all the days of my life, and I will dwell in the house of the LORD forever" (Psalm 23:6).

⁵¹ In Matthew 6:11, Jesus Christ said, "Give us this day our daily bread."

⁵² In Matthew 4:4, Jesus Christ said, "It is written: 'Man shall not live on bread alone, but on every word that comes from the mouth of God.'"

⁵³ In Matthew 6:33, Jesus Christ said, "Seek first the Kingdom of God and His righteousness and everything else will be added to you."

APRIL

⁵⁴ In Luke 21:36, Jesus Christ said, "But keep on the alert at all times, praying that you may have strength to escape all these things that are about to take place, and to stand before the Son of Man."

⁵⁵ In Psalm 57:1, the Psalmist wrote, "Be merciful unto me, O God, be merciful unto me, for my soul trusts in you. In the shadow of your wings will I make my refuge until these calamities pass by."

⁵⁶ "God and Father, who is over all and in all and living through all." (Ephesians 4:6).

⁵⁷ "For I can do everything through Christ, who gives me strength" (Philippians 4:13).

⁵⁸ In Matthew 6:33, Jesus Christ said, "Seek the Kingdom of God above all else, and live righteously, and he will give you everything you need."

⁵⁹ "Now to him who is able to do far more abundantly than all that we ask or think, according to the power at work within us" (Ephesians 3:20).

⁶⁰ In Mark 11:24, Jesus Christ said, "Therefore I tell you, whatever you ask in prayer, believe that you have received it, and it will be yours."

⁶¹ "The LORD your God is with you, the Mighty Warrior who saves. He will take

great delight in you; in his love he will no longer rebuke you, but will rejoice over you with singing" (Zephaniah 3:17).

⁶² "And my God will supply every need of yours according to his riches in glory in Christ Jesus" (Philippians 4:19).

⁶³ In Matthew 7:24-27, Jesus Christ said, "Everyone then who hears these words of mine and does them will be like a wise man who built his house on the rock. And the rain fell, and the floods came, and the winds blew and beat on that house, but it did not fall, because it had been founded on the rock. And everyone who hears these words of mine and does not do them will be like a foolish man who built his house on the sand. And the rain fell, and the floods came, and the winds blew and beat against that house, and it fell, and great was the fall of it."

⁶⁴ "Humble yourselves before the Lord, and he will lift you up in honor" (James 4:10).

⁶⁵ "Finally, brothers and sisters, whatever is true, whatever is noble, whatever is right, whatever is pure, whatever is lovely, whatever is admirable—if anything is excellent or praiseworthy—think about such things" (Philippians 4:8).

⁶⁶ "I pray that the eyes of your heart may be enlightened in order that you may know the hope to which he has called you, the riches of his glorious inheritance in his holy people" (Ephesians 1:18).

⁶⁷ "You anoint my head with oil; my cup overflows" (Psalm 23:5).

⁶⁸ "The LORD your God is with you, the Mighty Warrior who saves. He will take great delight in you; in his love he will no longer rebuke you, but will rejoice over you with singing" (Zephaniah 3:17).

⁶⁹ "Jesus Christ is the same yesterday, today, and forevermore" (Hebrews 13:8).

⁷⁰ In Matthew 6:33, Jesus Christ said, "Seek first the Kingdom of God and His righteousness, and everything else will be added to you."

⁷¹ "Delight yourself in the LORD, and He will give you the desires of your heart" (Psalm 37:4).

⁷² "Surely your goodness and love will follow me, and I will dwell in the house of the LORD forever" (Psalm 23:6).

⁷³ "We have this hope as an anchor for the soul, firm and secure" (Hebrews 6:19).

⁷⁴ "Delight yourself in the LORD, and He will give you the desires of your heart" (Psalm 37:4).

MAY

⁷⁵ "I lift up my eyes to you, to you who sit enthroned in heaven" (Psalm 123:1).

⁷⁶ "By faith we understand that the universe was formed at God's command, so that what is seen was not made out of what was visible" (Hebrews 11:3).

[77] In Matthew 7:24-27, Jesus Christ said, "Everyone then who hears these words of mine and does them will be like a wise man who built his house on the rock. And the rain fell, and the floods came, and the winds blew and beat on that house, but it did not fall, because it had been founded on the rock."

[78] "Let us fix our eyes on Jesus, the pioneer and perfecter of faith" (Hebrews 12:2).

[79] "Through Jesus Christ, I can do all things" (Philippians 4:13).

[80] "Trust in the LORD your God with all your heart, and lean not on your own understanding" (proverbs 3:5).

[81] "Do not conform to the pattern of this world, but be transformed by the renewing of your mind" (Romans 12:2).

[82] "Now to him who is able to do immeasurably more than all we ask or imagine, according to his power that is at work within us" (Ephesians 3:20).

[83] "May the God of hope fill you with all joy and peace as you trust in him, so that you may overflow with hope by the power of the Holy Spirit" (Romans 13:15).

[84] "For the LORD your God is with you, He will never leave you or forsake you" (Deuteronomy 31:6).

[85] "Delight yourself in the LORD, and He will give you the desires of your heart" (Psalm 37:4).

[86] In Matthew 6:34, Jesus Christ said, "Do not worry about tomorrow for tomorrow will worry about itself."

JUNE

[87] "A man reaps what he sows" (Galatians 6:7).

[88] The miracle of Jesus Christ feeding the multitudes is recorded in Matthew 14:13-21.

[89] In John 16:33, Jesus Christ said, "I have told you these things, so that in me you may have peace. In this world you will have trouble. But take heart! I have overcome the world."

[90] In Matthew 6:33, Jesus Christ said, "Seek first the Kingdom of God and His righteousness, and everything else will be added to you."

[91] This thought was shaped in my mind through a combination of the work of James Allen, Viktor Frankl, and Psalm 1.

[92] "That person is like a tree planted by streams of water, which yields its fruit in season, and whose lead foes not wither – whatever they do prospers" (Psalm 1:3).

[93] "But those who hope in the LORD will renew their strength. They will soar on wings like eagles; they will run and not grow weary, they will walk and not be faint" (Isaiah 40:31).

[94] "Jesus Christ is the same today, yesterday, and forever" (Hebrews 13:8).

[95] In Matthew 6:33, Jesus Christ said, "Seek first the Kingdom of God and His righteousness, and everything else will be added to you."

[96] This idea and imagery was formed in my mind through the work of B.K.S. Iyengar in his book, *Light on Life: The Yoga Journey to Wholeness, Inner Peace, and Ultimate Freedom* (Iyengar Yoga Books), September 19, 2006.

[97] "Surely your goodness and love will follow me all the days of my life, and I will dwell in the house of the LORD forever" (Psalm 23:6).

[98] "Rejoice always, pray continually, give thanks in all circumstances; for this is God's will for you in Christ Jesus" 1 Thessalonians 5:16-18

JULY

[99] "The prayer of a righteous person is powerful and effective" (James 5:6).

[100] "But Jesus immediately said to them: 'Take courage! It is I. Don't be afraid'" (Matthew 14:27).

[101] "Delight yourself in the LORD and He will give you the desires of your heart" (Psalm 37:4).

[102] In John 10:30, Jesus Christ said, "I and the Father are one."

[103] In Matthew 6:33, Jesus Christ said, "Seek first the Kingdom of God and His righteousness, and everything else will be added to you."

[104] In Matthew 6:34, Jesus Christ said, "Therefore do not worry about tomorrow, for tomorrow will worry about itself. Each day has enough trouble of its own."

[105] "Be still and know that I am God" (Psalm 46:10).

[106] In Matthew 6:33, Jesus Christ said, "Seek first the Kingdom of God and His righteousness, and everything else will be added to you."

[107] "Be still and know that I am God" (Psalm 46:10).

[108] "And after the earthquake a fire, but the LORD was not in the fire; and after the fire a still small voice" (1 Kings 19:12).

[109] "You have searched me LORD, and you know me" (Psalm 139:1).

[110] "You know when I sit and when I rise, you perceive my thoughts from afar" (Psalm 139:2).

[111] "I can do all things in Christ who strengthens me" (Philippians 4:13).

[112] "After John was put in prison, Jesus went into Galilee, proclaiming the good news of God" (John 1:14).

[113] "Your kingdom come, your will be done, on earth as it is in heaven" (Matthew 6:10).

[114] "But my God shall supply all your need according to his riches in glory by Christ Jesus" (Philippians 4:19).

[115] In Matthew 6:33, Jesus Christ said, "Seek first the Kingdom of God, and everything else will be added to you."

AUGUST

[116] "Surely your goodness and love will follow me all the days of my life, and I will dwell in the house of the LORD forever" (Psalm 23:6).

[117] "The Lord your God is with you, the Mighty Warrior who saves. He will take great delight in you; in his love he will no longer rebuke you, but will rejoice over you with singing" (Zephaniah 3:17).

[118] "I can do all things in Christ who strengthens me" (Philippians 4:13).

[119] "He leads me along the right paths for His name's sake" (Psalm 23:3).

[120] A Jewish Rabbi shared this version of the account of Moses parting the read sea with me. The purpose of the story was to highlight the faith that Moses had in God. Moses was prepared to continue into the sea until God answered him.

[121] "Surely your goodness and love will follow me all the days of my life, and I will dwell in the house of the LORD forever" (Psalm 23:6).

[122] "'Believe in the light while you have the light, so that you may become children of light.' When he had finished speaking, Jesus left and hid himself from them" (John 12:36).

[123] "For our light and momentary troubles are achieving for us an eternal glory that far outweighs them all" (2 Corinthians 4:17).

[124] "Trust in the LORD with all your heart, and lean not on your own understanding" (Proverbs 3:5).

[125] "But blessed is the one who trusts in the LORD, whose confidence is in him" (Jeremiah 17:7).

SEPTEMBER

[126] In the Gospel of Mark, Jesus Christ said, "Be on guard! Be alert! You do not know when the time will come" (Mark 10:33).

[127] "I will take refuge in the shadow of your wings until the disaster has passed" (Psalm 57:1).

[128] "The LORD will fight for you; you need only to be still" (Exodus 14:14).

[129] "In the Gospel of Luke, Jesus Christ said, "Nor will people say, 'Here it is,' or 'There it is,' because the kingdom of God is in your midst" (Luke 17:21).

[130] "But those who hope in the LORD will renew their strength. They will soar

on wings like eagles; they will run and not grow weary, they will walk and not be faint" (Isaiah 40:31).

[131] "What goes into someone's mouth does not defile them, but what comes out of their mouth, that is what defiles them" (Matthew 15:11).

[132] In the Gospel of Matthew, Jesus Christ said, "Seek the Kingdom of God above all else, and live righteously, and He will give you everything you need" (Matthew 6:33).

[133] Ibid.

[134] "Finally, brothers and sisters, whatever is true, whatever is noble, whatever is right, whatever is pure, whatever is lovely, whatever is admirable – if anything is excellent or praiseworthy – think about such things" (Philippians 4:8).

[135] "Surely your goodness and love will follow me all the days of my life, and I will dwell in the house of the LORD forever" (Psalm 23:6).

[136] "Jesus Christ is the same yesterday, and today, and forever" (Hebrews 13:8).

[137] "Now to him who is able to do immeasurably more than all we ask or imagine, according to his power that is at work within us" (Ephesians 3:20).

[138] "As the heavens are higher than the earth, so are my ways higher than your ways, and my thoughts than your thoughts" (Isaiah 55:9).

[139] "The LORD will fight for you; you need only to be still" (Exodus 14:14).

[140] "A good man brings good things out of the good stored up in his heart, and an evil man brings evil things out of the evil stored up in his heart. For the mouth speaks what the heart is full of" (Luke 6:45).

[141] In the Gospel of Matthew, Jesus Christ said, "Seek the Kingdom of God above all else, and live righteously, and He will give you everything you need" (Matthew 6:33).

OCTOBER

[142] In the Gospel of Matthew, Jesus Christ said, "If you believe, you will receive whatever you ask for in prayer" (Matthew 21:22).

[143] "I can do all things through Christ who strengthens me" (Philippians 4:13).

[144] This idea was formed in my mind through the work of B.K.S. Iyengar in his book, *Light on Life: The Yoga Journey to Wholeness, Inner Peace, and Ultimate Freedom* (Iyengar Yoga Books), September 19, 2006.

[145] In the Gospel of John, Jesus Christ said, "I have told you these things, so that in me you may have peace. In this world you will have trouble. But take heart! I have overcome the world" (John 16:33).

[146] "Today is the day the Lord has made; We will rejoice and be glad in it" (Psalm 118:24).

147 In the Gospel of Matthew, Jesus Christ said, "But store up for yourselves treasures in heaven, where moths and vermin do not destroy, and where thieves do not break in and steal. For where your treasure is, there your heart will be also" (Matthew 6:20-21).

148 In the Gospel of Matthew, Jesus Christ said, "Seek the Kingdom of God above all else, and live righteously, and He will give you everything you need" (Matthew 6:33).

149 "But my God shall supply all your need according to his riches in glory by Christ Jesus" (Philippians 4:19).

150 "Finally, brothers and sisters, whatever is true, whatever is noble, whatever is right, whatever is pure, whatever is lovely, whatever is admirable—if anything is excellent or praiseworthy—think about such things" (Philippians 4:8).

151 In the Gospel of Matthew, Jesus Christ said, "But blessed are your eyes, for they see: and your ears, for they hear" (Matthew 13:16).

152 "And after the earthquake a fire, but the Lord was not in the fire; and after the fire a still small voice" (1 Kings 19:12).

153 In the Gospel of Matthew, Jesus Christ said, "But I tell you, do not resist an evil person. If anyone slaps you on the right cheek, turn to them the other cheek also" (Matthew 5:39).

154 "And we know that in all things God works for the good of those who love him, who have been called according to his purpose" (Romans 8:28).

NOVEMBER

155 "But as for me, it is good to be near God. I have made the Sovereign LORD my refuge; I will tell of all your deeds" (Psalm 73:28).

156 In the Gospel of Luke, Jesus Christ said, "Nor will people say, 'Here it is,' or 'There it is,' because the kingdom of God is in your midst" (Luke 17:21).

157 "We are holding onto the hope of God's promise, which is an anchor for the soul, firm and secure" (Hebrews 10:25).

158 "Trust in the Lord with all your heart, and lean not on your own understanding; in all your ways submit to him, and he will make your paths straight" (Proverbs 3:6).

159 "But my God shall supply all your need according to his riches in glory by Christ Jesus" (Philippians 4:9).

160 "Jesus Christ the same yesterday, and today, and forever" (Hebrews 13:8).

161 In the Gospel of Matthew, Jesus Christ said, "Seek the Kingdom of God above all else, and live righteously, and He will give you everything you need" (Matthew 6:33).

¹⁶² "Trust in him at all times, you people; pour out your hearts to him, for God is our refuge" (Psalm 62:8).

¹⁶³ "You shall not fear them, for it is the Lord your God who fights for you" (Deuteronomy 3:22).

¹⁶⁴ "Now faith is the substance of things hoped for, the evidence of things not seen" (Hebrews 11:1).

¹⁶⁵ "The fear of the LORD is the beginning of wisdom, and knowledge of the Holy One is understanding" (Proverbs 9:10).

¹⁶⁶ "Therefore do not worry about tomorrow, for tomorrow will worry about itself. Each day has enough trouble of its own" (Matthew 6:34).

¹⁶⁷ "Commit to the LORD whatever you do, and he will establish your plans" (Proverbs 16:3).

DECEMBER

¹⁶⁸ "But you, Lord, are a shield around me, my glory, the One who lifts my head high" (Psalm 3:3).

¹⁶⁹ "You, dear children, are from God and have overcome them, because the one who is in you is greater than the one who is in the world" (1 John 4:4).

¹⁷⁰ "And my God will supply every need of yours according to his riches in glory in Christ Jesus" (Philippians 4:19).

¹⁷¹ "Wait for the LORD; be strong and take heart and wait for the LORD" (Psalm 27:14).

¹⁷² "Today is the day the LORD has made; let us rejoice and be glad in it" (Psalm 118:24).

¹⁷³ "For our light and momentary troubles are achieving for us an eternal glory that far outweighs them all" (2 Corinthians 4:17).

¹⁷⁴ "Jesus answered, 'If you want to be perfect, go, sell your possessions and give to the poor, and you will have treasure in heaven. Then come, follow me'" (Matthew 19:21).

¹⁷⁵ "And my God will supply every need of yours according to his riches in glory in Christ Jesus" (Philippians 4:19).

¹⁷⁶ "A new command I give you: Love one another. As I have loved you, so you must love one another" (John 13:34).

¹⁷⁷ "For in the same way you judge others, you will be judged, and with the measure you use, it will be measured to you" (Matthew 7:2).

¹⁷⁸ "Therefore I tell you, whatever you ask for in prayer, believe that you have received it, and it will be yours" (Mark 11:24).

¹⁷⁹ "Ask and it will be given to you; seek and you will find; knock and the door will be opened to you" (Matthew 7:7).

¹⁸⁰ "Do you not know that your bodies are temples of the Holy Spirit, who is in you, whom you have received from God?" (1 Corinthians 6:19).

¹⁸¹ "Finally, brothers and sisters, whatever is true, whatever is noble, whatever is right, whatever is pure, whatever is lovely, whatever is admirable—if anything is excellent or praiseworthy—think about such things" (Philippians 4:8).

¹⁸² "Jesus Christ the same yesterday, and today, and forever" (Hebrews 13:8).

¹⁸³ In the Gospel of Matthew, Jesus Christ said, "Seek the Kingdom of God above all else, and live righteously, and He will give you everything you need" (Matthew 6:33).

¹⁸⁴ "So is my word that goes out from my mouth: It will not return to me empty, but will accomplish what I desire and achieve the purpose for which I sent it" (Isaiah 55:11).

¹⁸⁵ "That person is like a tree planted by streams of water, which yields its fruit in season and whose leaf does not wither – whatever they do prospers" (Psalm 1:3).

¹⁸⁶ "And when he was demanded of the Pharisees, when the kingdom of God should come, he answered them and said, 'The kingdom of God cometh not with observation: Neither shall they say, Lo here! or, lo there! for, behold, the kingdom of God is within you'" (Luke 17:20-21).

¹⁸⁷ "Surely your goodness and love will follow me all the days of my life, and I will dwell in the house of the LORD forever" (Psalm 23:6).

¹⁸⁸ "Out of the abundance of the heart the mouth speaks" (Matthew 12:34).

¹⁸⁹ In the Gospel of Matthew, Jesus Christ said, "Seek the Kingdom of God above all else, and live righteously, and He will give you everything you need" (Matthew 6:33).

¹⁹⁰ "Finally, brothers and sisters, whatever is true, whatever is noble, whatever is right, whatever is pure, whatever is lovely, whatever is admirable—if anything is excellent or praiseworthy—think about such things" (Philippians 4:8).

¹⁹¹ "The LORD will fight for you, you need only to be still" (Exodus 14:14).

¹⁹² In the Gospel of Matthew, Jesus Christ said, "Seek the Kingdom of God above all else, and live righteously, and He will give you everything you need" (Matthew 6:33).

¹⁹³ "Pray continually, give thanks in all circumstances; for this is God's will for you in Christ Jesus" (1 Thessalonians 5:17).

Made in the USA
San Bernardino, CA
20 April 2019